Wednesday's PLACE

JOURNEY OF GRACE

WEDNESDAY GRACE

WESTBOW
PRESS®
A DIVISION OF THOMAS NELSON
& ZONDERVAN

New Living Translation (NLT) Holy Bible, New Living
Translation, copyright © 1996, 2004, 2015 by Tyndale House
Foundation. Used by permission of Tyndale House Publishers
Inc., Carol Stream, Illinois 60188. All rights reserved.

New Life Version (NLV) Copyright © 1969 by
Christian Literature International

WestBow Press books may be ordered through
booksellers or by contacting:

WestBow Press
A Division of Thomas Nelson & Zondervan
1663 Liberty Drive
Bloomington, IN 47403
www.westbowpress.com
1 (866) 928-1240

ISBN: 978-1-9736-0178-4 (sc)
ISBN: 978-1-9736-0179-1 (e)

Library of Congress Control Number: 2017913945

Print information available on the last page.

WestBow Press rev. date: 09/18/2017

Special Thank You!

Robin, I am so thankful for all of your help with this story. I never would have found enough courage to share my story without your support. Thank you for helping me with editing and bible verses. You are a true "Mighty Woman of God!"

When I first began this story twelve years ago, my purpose was to write my memories down so I did not have to carry them on my shoulders anymore. I did not want to think about the pain and hurt I had endured. Writing down my story allowed me to let go! Over the years, I have thought about Wednesday's Child and her place in this crazy world. If sharing my challenges can help others see how God is love and He does care about us, then it was worth the pain I endured.

As I share my story, I do not want to come across as if I am saying that my parents were not good. They were both hardworking and creative, and they showed me so much love. I do want to show how hate can destroy a family.

ಶಿ Child of Woe

I have a picture that used to hang in my bedroom. It is a picture of seven little girls—one for each day of the week. Each is dressed in a fancy Victorian-style dress. I was born on a Wednesday. The picture reads, "Wednesday's child is a child of woe." What does this mean? Who am I supposed to be? How am I supposed to act? What am

I supposed to do with my life? I looked up the word *woe*. It means "great sorrow or grief, misfortune." No wonder I've had so many challenges. I was born on the wrong day of the week! Or was I?

∞ Unwanted but Wanted

My biological mother and father chose to give me up for adoption.

> Can a woman forget her nursing child? Can she have no pity on the son (daughter) to whom she gave birth? Even these may forget, but I will not forget you. See, I have marked your names on My hands. Your walls are always before Me. (Isaiah 49:15–16 NLV)

> My bones were not hidden from You when I was made in secret and put together with care in the deep part of the earth. Your eyes saw me before I was put together. And all the days of my life were written in Your book before any of them came to be. (Psalm 139:15–16 NLV)

I was adopted when I was seven days old. A nice woman took care of me those first seven days of my little life. She wrote a short journal documenting how I ate, how I slept, and how I behaved. Her words were very kind. She said I was a perfect baby. To this day, I still try to live up to her words—*perfect*.

My new parents were a creative pair! My mom grew up in the Lutheran Church. She came from a broken, unstable home with too many heartbreaking issues. She made some wrong choices and tried to hide behind lies. Piles and piles of lies. My dad grew up in the Mormon Church. He came from a broken family that was suffering from alcoholism and anger. My new mom and dad had been married for thirteen years. Their marriage was not healthy; instead, it was full of unresolved childhood wounds and issues. They tried to have a baby, but they miscarried.

This was Dad's second marriage. He had an older son from his first marriage. I did not grow up around my stepbrother. He spent most of my childhood in and out of detention centers. They had another child who died of SIDS. I never knew her name.

Mom would always tell me stories about how hard she had prayed for a little girl. She already had the nursery decorated in yellow-and-white gingham check. The closet was full of beautiful, frilly dresses and ruffled socks just waiting for the perfect baby girl to wear.

On the other hand, my dad, a full-blooded Irishman, did not want anything to do with a half-breed—and certainly not a girl! I think it was because he had already lost his little girl. His heart was broken.

Well, on a day in the middle of December, a little half-English, half-Native American girl was born in Reno! They both tell happy stories about the day they got me from a Mormon adoption agency. One winter morning Mom picked up the phone, not knowing that call would change her life. Crazy with excitement, she called for Dad, but Dad was in the middle of an important construction job. He was pouring some concrete for a new bank vault in Vegas, and they would not let Mom see me until Dad got there. Dad was the first one to hold me. He says something inside of him changed that day. All the stories I have heard about that day have always made me feel special. They called me the rent-a-kid!

ಬಿ The Rent-a-Kid's Struggle with Perfection Begins

> I was in Your care from birth. Since my mother gave birth to me, You have been my God. Do not be far from me, for trouble is near. And there is no one to help. (Psalm 22:10–11 NLV)

Well, my job began. They called me a perfect baby. I was always clean, and I slept like an angel. Dad said he wanted to take me to the doctor; he thought there was something wrong with me because I would never cry. My mom says I was perfect until I turned eight years old. That deeply hurt me. I tried so hard not to mess up. I hated to get in trouble.

As I grew up, I tried very hard to be my dad's tomboy, knowing he did not want a girl. I would try not to let myself like the color pink, which was a girl's color, or play with frilly girl toys. I loved playing with balls—big, giant balls; small balls; and brightly colored balls! Give me a bouncy ball, and I could be entertained for hours. I would throw bouncy balls on the roof of the house, bounce balls hard on the driveway to see how high they could go, or play catch if someone was around to play. I would always ask for a quarter when we would go to the grocery store so I could get a small crazy-colored rubber ball. I had every kind!

On my third birthday, I got my first motorized three-wheeler. It was bright yellow with my name written in cobalt-blue cursive on the side. I had a matching helmet with a little visor to keep the sun out of my eyes. My first time driving my new vehicle of freedom, I brushed the side of the wooden gate where you would enter our property. I smashed my right hand, turned back with tears in my eyes, and looked at my dad. Mom was angry that Dad had bought a three-year-old girl something so dangerous. I loved that three-wheeler.

Our house was on the outskirts of Vegas. I had a great big desert area to race around. I would drive around in our backyard, dodging danger and jumping speed bumps. One day, Dad interviewed me with his video camera. He asked me what I liked to do. I said something about going up and down and around and around real fast. When I outgrew my three-wheeler, I took over my dad's brand-new four-wheeler. He had to go buy another matching red-and-blue four-wheeler for himself. I liked his because it was faster and you could push a button to start the motor; on mine, you had to pull a hard, black rope. Thank God for technology!

I have blocked out many of my childhood memories, but looking back at the times I went four-wheeling on dirt trails, overcoming childhood fears by my house, and bringing Cabbage Patch dolls out on the trails to play house with a close friend makes me laugh.

Sometimes on the weekends at our getaway home in the beautiful, red rock mountains of Utah, Dad would gas up the four-wheelers and pack a lunch, and we would head out for a day trip. He was always in front, and I would follow behind and eat his dust—praying not to crash or get lost.

> I will lift up my eyes to the mountains. Where will my help come from? My help comes from the Lord, Who made heaven and earth. He will not let your feet go out from under you. He Who watches over you will not sleep. (Psalm 121:1–3 NLV)

One day I did lose sight of him. We were driving through a mountain area. It was so dusty, and I could not see him. There was a fork in the dirt road, and I was not sure which way he had gone. I got scared and started crying; I stopped and started praying to God for Dad to find me. When he did find me, he hugged me as we both cried.

On another one of our crazy adventures, it started to rain very hard, so Dad found an old, abandoned camper that sheepherders would have used. We camped out in it for a couple of hours as we waited for the rain to let up. That was crazy!

Dad went through many ranch hands at our ranch in the mountains. He had a Spanish ranch hand who did not speak much English. This brave man accompanied us one summer on a Sunday afternoon for a four-wheeler ride. Dad would go up some pretty steep trails. I learned you had to put the four-wheeler in low gear and pray you would not slide backward. Well, the ranch hand did not understand what to do. He was following behind me on the old orange hand-me-down, hard-rope-pulling four-wheeler that I passed up. As we were going up the side of a steep mountain, I saw our ranch hand disappear. I rode up to Dad and said, "I think he's fallen off the side of the mountain!" Dad said some choice words and went back to find the poor guy. Sure enough, he rolled off the side of the mountain and landed in a tree.

Dad says when he found the poor man, the ranch hand said, "Please, mister, let me rest here and get my heart started." He was roughed up, but he had survived our Sunday drive! I am thankful it was not me rolling off the hill and causing conflict. On those trips with Dad, I spent a lot of time praying I would not mess up or crash. You can say those experiences drew me closer to God!

> He who lives in the safe place of the
> Most High will be in the shadow of the

All-powerful. ² I will say to the Lord, "You are my safe and strong place, my God, in Whom I trust." (Psalm 91:1–2 NLV)

ೞ You Might Say to Yourself, "She Is Weird!"

The head man said to him, "Everyone puts out his best wine first. After people have had much to drink, he puts out the wine that is not so good. You have kept the good wine until now!" (John 2:10 NLV)

I was a weird child. I would save the best for last: the best candies, the best stickers, the best colors. I remember one time I was with my mom and my grandma, traveling back from Texas. As usual, after eating, Mom had to make an emergency stop on the side of the road. I had a small, brand-new package of pastel-colored tissues. Mom really needed to use them! I would give her one tissue at a time. I slowly handed her the yellow tissues first, then the green ones, and then the blue tissues. She got really upset and yelled at me, "Give me the whole … pack of tissues!"

With only the pretty pink ones left, I got so upset and cried out, "Mom you are using all my pink tissues!" My grandma, sitting in the front passenger seat, started laughing so hard. I gave my mom all my tissues in her time of need. Even the pink ones!

My grandma, for years, loved to retell the pink tissue story. She would start laughing and say, "Please don't take my pink tissues!"

To continue my weird habits, I would save my money. My cousins would waste their money on candy or foolish toys. I would always save mine. When I got older, I would iron my money so it was nice and flat and put it in order, all facing the same direction. Then I would hide it under the carpet in the corner of my room. Goofy, I know!

When I was about five years old, my mom and I went into an art supply store. We were walking down each aisle, looking at all the pretty supplies, and my eyes were captured by these pretty white thumb tacks stamped with bright, colorful butterflies. I really wanted those soft, puffy butterfly thumbtacks. They were so pretty. When I asked Mom, she said, "No!" I don't know why, but I felt I needed them, so I committed my first crime! I don't remember how I got them to the car; I just remember hiding them under the back seat in our burgundy and tan Ford Bronco II. Then, after what seemed like an eternity but was only a couple minutes later, I pulled them out from under the back seat and said, "Mom, look what I found!" She yelled out my name, pressed on the brakes, jerked the car around, and sped back to the store. Grabbing me by the arm, she marched me right back into the store and made me confess. Let's just say that since that dark day, I have never had the desire to buy any type of pretty, puffy thumbtacks, and I certainly have not had the desire to shoplift. I was so ashamed! Why would I do that? There went another strike against my perfection.

> Anyone who steals must stop it! He must work with his hands so he will have what he needs and can give to those who need help. (Ephesians 4:28 NLV)

∞ Creative Friendship

I had a friend next door; she was a couple of years older than me. We were a creative pair. We became business partners. We created a bakery. Our location was an old stable for horses in my backyard. We took orders for all types of delicate pastries made from the finest mud the West could offer! We were very serious about our business. We used my mom's pie pans and cooking utensils. We had notepads to write orders and to give receipts. We even had a white, fancy metal cart to roll our pastries on for display!

I did have some enemies in my backyard; they were white and gray, had long necks, and would pinch me with their beaks. Yes, they were scary, mean geese! They would poop all over our back porch. I felt like a hostage in my own house. I would have to look out the back door to check to see if the coast was clear to go outside to play. I was very afraid of them. They had friends too! Their friends had feathers also. They lived in a chicken coop. I was supposed to go in their pen to collect eggs. They were not very giving. They would fly all over the place. Sometimes they would get their claws stuck in my dark, puffy, permed hair. I was very scared of the feathered family growing up. Let's just say they were not welcomed at our bakery!

✂ Blessed with Talent

My mother was a talented decorator. She would decorate houses for political figures and wealthy business owners. She organized all kinds of parties, including weddings. She was very creative, but her faults got the best of her. Her painful childhood would not let her go. She lived in a world of lies. She was captured by hatred. I was so proud of her talent; I wanted to be a decorator just like her! I would lay stretched out on the floor and look through her huge, thick decorating books, studying what colors and patterns should go together. When she would hang pictures or decorate a room, I would watch and study the arrangements. Sometimes I would ask questions. She would say, "You either have it or you don't." I wanted so badly to please her but could not. She would always say, "If you only knew how much I love you." I would try so hard to prove my love to her. I understand now why, but as a child, I did not understand that because of her childhood pain, she did not have the ability to receive love.

As mentioned before, my parents' marriage was not very stable or loving. I believe they adopted me to try to fix their marriage. They would fight all the time. I remember one time it got very bad. I was probably around five years old. It was late at night. The arguing had gotten intense. My mom told me to go pack my bags. As a young child, I did not worry about my clothes or shoes, only my toys and coloring books! I sat on the floor in the corner by the front door with my backpack full of toys, crying, listening to them fight, waiting to leave. Their fights got very heated: walls kicked, keys thrown, doors punched. My mom's sister thought she was helping and turned them into the family services. That did not help much. My mom and dad got very angry with her. Mom completely disowned my aunt for many years.

> And I say, "If only I had wings like a dove,
> I would fly away and be at rest. (Psalm
> 55:6 NLV)

೮೦ Start with One and Build Your Way Up!

One day, my dad came home with a used, red, one-ton crane. My mom was not too crazy about the idea, but Dad had a vision, a plan. Our crane company challenges began. The new office moved into the family den at our ranch style home. Office hours were from five o'clock in the morning until five o'clock at night. I was expected to be quiet while anyone was on the telephone or on the CB radio. As an only child with a tan-colored cocker spaniel dog as my playmate, I learned to entertain myself. Cuddles the cocker learned how to play dress-up and ride in a baby doll stroller. He was a good friend.

One crane turned into two cranes, then three cranes and then more. This risk started to pay off! I remember always having these big cranes parked in our backyard where I would ride my three-wheeler. The crane operators became a part of our family. My birthday would also be the company Christmas party! Mom would always overdo it with pony rides, hundreds of balloons, and clowns, and, of course, Mr. and Mrs. Santa would always stop by! I would always get such nice presents from the employees, family, and friends. One year I was able to invite some girls from school. They were girls who liked dolls and dresses. Well, remember me, Miss Tomboy. Mom had given our employees suggestions on what gifts I would like. As I opened each gift and all these dump trucks and balls started to appear, these new friends said, "You like trucks?" I lied and said, "No!" I was embarrassed, and my mom was upset too because she had recommended these gifts.

> So stop lying to each other. Tell the truth to your neighbor. We all belong to the same body. (Ephesians 4:25 NLV)

What do you think was the first toy I played with after everyone left the party? Yes, my trucks, and I went out in the mud in my pretty, frilly dress and ruffled socks and got quite dirty! There again, I was acting how I thought someone wanted me to act, pretending to be someone I was not.

⋯ How Much Should One Sacrifice for Success?

My dad's business expanded. He built an office at another location and hired a secretary. The office became my second home. I would go there every day after school.

My dad, who seemed to be made out of strong, tough, Irish tempered steel, was being challenged by a certain local construction group. They would stand outside the tall chain-link gates that surrounded a large, desert, landscaped lot. A tall, two-story office made out of large, gray bricks stood in the center of the fenced-in property. Protesters with signs would spend all day yelling mean words as people entered the property. This group of people would also show up at job sites and wave picket signs, yelling hateful sayings as Dad's crane operators would try to work. I was very scared and worried. This group physically beat Dad one day when he came to check on his crane operators at a job site.

My dad, who liked things nice, clean and in order, used to have the crane operators line the cranes up side by side in a nice, straight row each night when everyone was finished working for the day. One day when Dad came to the office at 5:30 in the morning, all his cranes were lying on their sides like giant, crashed dominos. Someone, an enemy, had used one of the booms of a crane like a medieval, spiked ball on a large chain and swung the boom to hit the side of the crane sending the other cranes down like dominos, one by one.

Business got personal when my life was threatened. I remember when I was in kindergarten of being taken out of private school by officials and hidden. I was very scared. During that same time frame, I remember my family coming home from dinner one dark night. Driving through the same gate where I had smashed my hand while riding my three-wheeler, I saw this strange man in dark clothes, his face covered in a mask, running out of our front door. He disappeared into the dark, scary night. We had been robbed, but not much was stolen. They were looking for business information. I remember running into my room and checking to see if any of my things were missing. I counted all my coloring books; one was missing! I was very talented in coloring. I guess they could not resist my artwork! The next day, an alarm system was installed. That did not stop us from being robbed again and again. That was a scary time. Dad had late-night meetings at the office with wires hidden, bomb threats, and information at risk!

So let us recap. I was adopted when I was seven days old. I was a perfect baby. My parents did not have a healthy marriage. I committed my first crime at the age of five years old. We were victims of robbery; lives were threatened. I owned my first bakery, and my mom used all of my pink tissues! Just think, all this happened before the age of eight. You would think life would get better. No, my next eight years would be a miserable nightmare. I call it my family's World War lll.

౭ **My Family's World War III Begins**.

When I was eight, my so-called secure world turned upside down. This large cloud of hate came over my family and would not leave. My dad left my mom. The war of divorce began. I remember my mom would take all this medication: pills to sleep, pills to wake up, pills to eat, pills to stop her crying, and who knows what else. She cried all the time. She would not get dressed to take me to school. When she would pick me up from school, she would still be in her pajamas. She would cry in her bed or lie on the couch and watch TV all day. I learned how to do laundry and clean the house. I taught myself how to cook things like mac and cheese, microwave dinners, and ramen noodles. A healthy meal would be cantaloupe with cottage cheese. She would drive through a fast-food joint, and we would order a cheeseburger and fries for most of our lunches and dinners.

Depression took my mom to a deep, dark place where she was not living—just existing. I became the mother, and she became the child. We would argue about Dad. She would always have to tell me all the horrible things that he was supposedly doing to her. She would say she was dying from some disease one week and cancer another week. This caused anger to grow inside of me, an anger so deep and frustrating.

❧ Everyone Should Have an Aunt Molly!

Aunt Molly had three children. I was closest to Jean. She was much older than I was. I wanted to be her little sister so badly. Jim was in the middle. He was so smart; he had no fear and got in trouble often. Jane was three months younger than I was. We were like night and day. She was jealous of my relationship with her sister Jean. We would argue about everything. When we would play Barbies, I would just want to dress them and do their hair. She would want to play pretend. I would want to play ball, and she would want to play house. We would compromise and play games like Uno or Parcheesi. It was safe at Molly's house—no tension.

I started to grow closer to my mom's mother and my Aunt Molly. I wanted to spend as much time with them as possible. It was normal with them. A safe zone, empty of hate, anger, and stress. A predictable place, with no yelling, no crying.

Every Saturday, Aunt Molly and Grandma would go to garage sales. Sometimes I was lucky enough to tag along. We would stop and get a ham, egg, and cheese biscuit, orange juice, and a hash brown at our favorite fast-food joint. With the newspaper in hand, all garage sales circled, we would head out on a search for hidden "have to have" treasures. Then we would go back to Aunt Molly's house and sit in the kitchen. Molly would smoke a cigarette, and I would sit next to Grandma. She would play with my hair or take out her earring and check to see if my ears were still pierced.

✌ Vacations are not for Everyone!

I loved it when Grandma would tell stories about when I was a baby. She would take care of me when Mom and Dad would go on vacation. She was in charge of answering the company phone and watching me. She said she was always worried something bad would happen when they were gone. Like, I would get a bump on my head or something would go wrong with the business. She had good reason to be worried. One time, my stepbrother took my mom's van, which she used for her decorating business, out of the state for a joy ride! That did not go over too well when Mom and Dad got home!

Mom and Dad liked to go to Yellowstone in the winter to snowmobile with friends. I was too young to snowmobile alongside the buffalo. Therefore, they would bring me home souvenirs. One year I received an educational video on Old Faithful the geyser. Nice!

Mom talked Dad into going to Hawaii one year. Let's just say Hawaii is a little too small for Dad! He panicked in a helicopter while on a tour of the islands. On that same trip, Mom passed gallbladder stones in a jeep going across a bridge. Painful!

The only family trip I remember going on with my parents was to Washington, DC, and Hershey, Pennsylvania. I was almost run over by a yellow Corvette while crossing the road. If that was not scary enough, I got lost on the subway. On that same family vaction, we went to an Amish community. They had beautiful quilts and Amish buggies for sale. I remember little Amish kids riding scooters made completely out of wood. We ate in a great big Amish barn with big, long picnic tables lined up in rows full of people from all over. I remember getting very sick from eating too much homemade butterscotch pudding at the Amish supper. Oh yeah, and on the way home, I delayed the plane because I had toy handcuffs in my carry-on bag. A couple weeks after our exciting family trip, I found rotten yogurt that was left in my backpack. Memories!

✂ Hush little one, don't you cry!

I remember Grandma telling stories about when I would get hurt. She said I would not cry when I would bump my head or scrape my knees. I would hold in my tears inside as much as I could until I could not hold them any longer. Aunt Molly said she hates to hear me cry; she said it was too sad.

> You have seen how many places I have gone. Put my *tears* in Your bottle. Are they not in Your book? (Psalm 56:8 NLV)

I was not supposed to cry. I was supposed to be able to handle it, be strong and brave. I was supposed to be perfect. I would hold it all in, and then finally, like a dam holding back a lake of water, I would just break down, usually around Grandma or Aunt Molly, and cry. Then when the dam of tears broke, it was hard to stop; I would not be able to catch my breath. Tears would just pour out as I gasped for air. I miss my grandma and her green polyester pants and green-and-white polka-dotted blouse. She was always so gentle.

✂ Hate Will Destroy

> He will say to them, "Hear, O Israel. Today you are going into battle against those who

> hate you. Do not let your hearts become
> weak. Do not be afraid and shake in fear
> before them." (Deuteronomy 20:3 NLV)

My parents went to court to get a divorce. I was supposed to live with my mom and visit my dad every Wednesday and stay over every other weekend. I hated this arrangement. The day I was supposed to go with Dad, Mom would start an argument with me, accusing me of loving Dad more than her. She would always have to bring it up that Dad left her and caused her pain. She would say she helped create the crane and restaurant business and deserved half of both. She wanted me to hate him as much as she did. She was so hurt that he left. So angry. She never allowed herself to move on. It was as if she was in a movie, stuck in a moment, and was not able to fast forward to the present time.

When Dad would pick me up, he would be so angry. Mom usually had written a hateful letter or served him with some kind of lawsuit. He would vent his anger for her out on me. He would inform me how awful she was, how crazy, fat, and ugly she had become. He too had been consumed with this hate and anger. They both spent hundreds of thousands of dollars on legal fees and lawsuits. At first, Mom and I had moved to the family ranch house in the mountains. It was the middle of my third-grade year. I was behind on my reading skills. I was an overweight, knocked-kneed, pigeon-toed child who was very self-conscious about my appearance. In school,

I enjoyed math and kick ball at recess. I really struggled with reading and spelling.

ℰ Whoa, Little Lady, Let's Back Up!

I need to back up and mention some things. My parents fell in love with this small town hiding in the middle of the beautiful red rock mountains of Utah. They would drive two hours and forty-five minutes each Friday night, from Vegas, to stay for the weekends, even before I was born. At first, they would stay in a camper; then they bought this cute little house in town. I remember it being a gray, one-story house with a Jacuzzi. There were these boys across the street who would come over and tease me. We then moved into a gray tri-level house, which had very nice four-wheeling trails out behind the house. One dirt trail looked like a camel's humps, and one trail felt like you were in a toilet bowl. I spent many hours in the dust back there.

At first, I only had one friend in this small town. She would come over on Saturdays after she had finished her chores at home. We would play in a small stream across the street with inner tubes or haul our Cabbage Patch dolls out to the trails and ride four-wheelers and play house. You see, I got to play in the dirt and with dolls at the same time. Who knew you could combine the two?

We lived in that house until I was about six or seven. Then my parents built what they considered their dream home. It was a brick house with gray stucco and white trim. Yes, in the mountains, I only lived in gray houses! It had four bedrooms. Mom decorated it with light pink paint, different wallpapers hung in each room, and wainscoting. She had beige carpet trimmed with rose accents throughout the house. They had designed and created their dream home.

I had a cool room above the garage that had slanted walls. It was big, with a sitting room and an attached bathroom, all decorated with light pink and blue hearts. My room had two window seats. With this new house, I met a new friend too. My two friends and I would play fast-food restaurant. We would use the windows for drive-up service. We mostly sold plastic pizza and cheeseburgers. I had closed down the mud pie business. (Mom wouldn't allow mud pies in my bedroom.) There was a spring-fed pond in my front yard. It was full of red clay mud and koi, a type of fish. My friends and I would swim in the red, muddy pond in the summer and try to walk on the ice in the winter.

Shortly after we moved into our dream house, my parents built a restaurant and motel with a room used for banquets on the second floor. Mom organized and decorated for weddings and parties. The restaurant took up a lot of time and money. It added more stress to the already stressful life. Don't forget, they still had the crane company too! Mom designed and decorated homes and organized events, and now she took on a restaurant and hotel. Do you remember our crazy trip to Pennsylvania? They bought an Amish wagon and a paint horse to drive in parades and give rides to motel guests. Later they bought a team of Belgian horses and more wagons.

Well, Mom and I were supposed to move up to the ranch to take care of the restaurant and motel, but I believe it was because things were not stable. Dad was always stressed out about the crane business, and now this new resort was financially draining him. We moved up there in the middle of my third grade year. Dad would come up on the weekends.

I was never very social and was full of insecurity. My two friends were a year older than I was, so we were not in the same class. I remember my teacher was extremely athletic. She liked to play kickball. That was fun. I could not run fast, but I could kick the ball really far. I did not like baseball at recess. There was too much pressure to hit that small ball with a long, narrow bat and run to base before they tagged you out. No, it just was not for me. I liked basketball, and soccer was fun, but not baseball. School was hard for me. I tried hard; I really struggled in reading.

My mom always wanted me to learn how to play the piano because, in my adoption papers, it said my biological mother played the piano. When I was three or four years old, I was in a piano class where you played by hearing; that was not my gift. When I got older, my mom made me go to a piano teacher who handed out root beer barrel candies and gave out shining colored stars when I practiced my homework lessons. Well, it takes more than long fingers to play the piano. I did not have an ear for music, and the wires from my brain to my fingers were not installed yet! I did not have coordination at all. The only thing I learned was that it is not safe to stand on your piano books while trying to ride a scooter downhill. You will only slip off and get deep, gravel-scarred knees that will last forever.

∞ Thank God for Music! A Place to Escape.

At our new, family-owned, small-town restaurant and motel, there was this receptionist. She was a nice, pretty, Christian girl in college. I do not know why she took me to my first Sawyer Brown concert one night when I was nine, but I am very thankful that she did. I remember Mark Miller wearing these wild outfits and dancing crazily while singing "The Race Is On." I bought my first tape and T-shirt at that concert. I loved it. I now had an escape from this pain that was overflowing inside. I would lie on the floor in my sitting room and play my Sawyer Brown tape over and over. My favorite song was "Heart Don't Fall Now." I would play, rewind, and play that song over and over. Remember tapes? They were not as easy to rewind as CDs.

∞ How Many Times Can One Be Thrown off a Horse? Let Me Count the Ways!

You remember that paint horse I mentioned? Well, I thought I should become a cowgirl. Dad had a fancy western saddle made for me. It was beautiful. My riding lessons lasted about twenty minutes. I was then turned loose to ride the brown-and-white paint horse named

Indy. One day this little five-year-old girl with her pony asked if I wanted to go for a ride. She was so cute with her long, light-blonde hair, but she was tough as any boy. She knew so much more about riding than I did. We saddled up and headed to the fairgrounds. We entered the racetrack area and started to walk around the track. All of a sudden, Indy got upset and started running as fast as he could around the track. I got scared, dropped my split reins, and tried to hold on, screaming, "Please stop." Indy ran toward the railing and jumped over. I fell off, hitting my head on the way down. The last thing I remember is seeing Indy running out of the fairgrounds into the sunset. I woke up in a hospital. My dad came all the way from Vegas. He swears it only took him two hours to drive 172 miles! I spent the next week at home, throwing up and drinking apple juice. To this day, I cannot drink apple juice without thinking about that moment in my life.

You know the old saying, "If you fall off the horse, you get right back on." Well, I did not want to get back on that crazy horse, but my dad made me. I was full of fear but tried to hide it. My dad was driving a team of Belgian draft horses in a parade; Indy and I followed behind the wagon. Guess where the parade ended? Yes, at the same fairgrounds. I was very nervous. We did not go near the racetrack, but, as we walked, a rock hidden by dry grass, seemed to jump out and spooked Indy. And, yes, I did fall off again! Yes, I envisioned the same scene: Indy running out of the fairgrounds. My dad got upset at me. Well, you know the rule: get back on the horse. I did get back on; I did go back to the fairgrounds, and the same rock spooked Indy; I did not fall off this time! I almost did, but I held on. I do not know what happened to Indy at the fairgrounds, but something did. Maybe he had been hurt there before and did not want to relive that memory. I can relate. I have many memories I have blocked out. Trust me, there are a lot more I wish I could forget.

> No, Christian brothers, I do not have that life yet. But I do one thing. I forget everything that is behind me and look forward to that which is ahead of me. (Philippians 3:13 NLV)

I retired my saddle and learned how to drive a team of Belgian draft horses instead. Dad said I was going to be the best girl driver the draft horse world had ever seen. That was short-lived. I loved driving, but my parents' actions pushed me away from horses. Dad would make me very tense. He was always so uptight because of his businesses and the divorce that he would not be able to relax enough to enjoy the horses. We would be in a parade, and something small would go wrong; he would get upset. The joy was gone.

I remember a time when our restaurant and motel offered a wagon trail ride to our guests. My dad was in front, driving a wagon with a team of draft horses, and I followed, driving a real covered wagon. My team of horses, Annie and Molly, were sisters. Annie was brown with a blond mane. Molly was brown with a bright-red mane. She was my favorite. I felt safe around her. She would always run my way when she saw me coming. My covered wagon was full of French men singing "Home on the Range." As they sang, I was praying, "God, please bless me not to crash; please bless the horses not to run off." We went through some rough terrain, down into old riverbanks and up steep hills. After that adventure, Dad would brag to people about his twelve-year-old driving a wagon full of French men!

When I would come home from these adventures with Dad, Mom would cause a fight. She would cry, "I wanted the horses. Those are my horses. You don't love me because you had fun with your dad and the horses." It became very miserable. So, I pushed away from the horses. No more fighting with Mom over loving the horses more than her. No more tiptoeing around Dad at parades, trying not to make a mistake. Problem solved!

> They must not speak bad of anyone, and they must not argue. They should be gentle and kind to all people. (Titus 3:2 NLV)

∾ Mother, How Do Girls Act?

I believe God puts people in our lives at certain times when we need them the most. After my parents' divorce, my dad started to date a true Italian woman. I felt comfortable around her; she was very easy to talk with. She taught me how to cook. Because of her, I can make a pretty tasty homemade spaghetti sauce! She would always say to treat people how you would want to be treated. She showed me that Jesus is real. She taught me that it was okay to be a girl and to want to be pretty. I am thankful for the talks we had and time I spent with her. She made visits with Dad easier. She really wanted children but only had cats and a dog. I guess me being the rent-a-kid allowed her to rent me for a time!

When I came home from visiting Dad, my mom would always be upset. She would say, "I can't believe you like her. You love her more than me. Do you want her as your mother?" Are you starting to get the picture? I was reaching out to people because my parents were so caught up in this hate war; they could not see how it was affecting me. I did not help the matter. I closed up around both of them. I felt like a tennis ball being hit back and forth, each hit being harder and filled with more anger, trying to hurt one another. I was in the middle, and they were trying to make me hate the other as much as they did.

> Look after each other so that none of you fails to receive the grace of God. Watch out that no poisonous root of bitterness grows up to trouble you, corrupting many. (Hebrews 12:15 NLT)

✌ How Can One Be Taken from One's Own Home?

My parents fought over money, businesses, light fixtures, property, and their dream house in the mountains. The hate and anger became very scary. I do not know what caused the hostility between my mom and the tall, strong ranch hand hired by my dad, but I do remember watching my mom being beaten with a long 2x4 in the driveway of what was supposed to be the house my parents were to grow old in together. Yes, my mom was filled with uncontrollable anger, but no one deserves to be beaten, especially not in front of her child. That is a memory I try to block out. I still can see the large bruises on her legs and watching her try to crawl away. Shortly after the brawl, my mom and I were forced, by court order, to leave our dream home in the mountains. I remember a police car with flashing lights escorting us out of our driveway. My dad was too caught up in his hate for Mom to realize how this affected me.

We unwillingly moved back to Vegas. We didn't move back into the house that I grew up in; that house had been sold. This was a new house in a new housing development close to a scary, new school. My mother was still in her pink stage. She said the pale pink color was peaceful. The walls were pink, the carpet had rose accents, and the couches were pink with a floral print. My mom would take me to school in her pajamas each morning; she would pick me up from school in her pajamas each afternoon. I was so embarrassed. This motivated me to walk to school! When I walked home from school in the afternoon and mom was not home, I would crawl through the doggy door and rush to turn off the alarm system. Why use a key when you have a doggy door? I went to school in the city my sixth and seventh grade year after spending half of third, fourth, and fifth grade in a small town in the mountains.

Here we go again! I was the new kid in school. After being in a small town, I noticed the kids in the big city were different: different attitudes, different judgments, different challenges to face. I liked living in a small town. I liked my small school. Now, I was just another fish in a big pond: lost, swimming in the deep end.

ဆ Off to Grandmother's House We Go!

When I was thirteen, my mom let me go spend the summer with my grandma in a small, Texan oil town where she had been raised. I had the best time. I arrived in this small, peaceful town and fell in love with it—not the town as much as the stress-free air, the non-angry water, and the warm, loving sun!

Grandma would get up early every morning, put on her pink-and-white housecoat, and make a pot of coffee. We would sit at the kitchen table and eat cornflakes and drink half coffee, half milk and sugar. Grandma would tell me stories about her childhood. She would talk about only getting a new dress and a new pair of shoes at Easter time. She said they would have to last until Christmas. She talked about the times of war and depression. She explained how supplies like flour and sugar had to be rationed each month. I could listen to her stories all day.

After breakfast, Grandma and I would get dressed and go work at the gas station and detail shop that my grandpa was leasing. I would wash and detail cars and big oil trucks. Grandpa would say I was good but slow. I was a perfectionist. I would make sure every little piece of dirt was out of the carpet and every spot was dried. Yeah, I know, I was obsessed with cleaning; just add it to my list!

After dinner on Saturday nights, Grandma and I would drive downtown to the local ice cream shop for a chocolate-covered ice cream bar and a peanut butter shake. I wish I could have frozen that time with her in my heart and just live in it forever. I understand the importance of grandparents. She filled my heart with the comfort and peace I so deeply needed.

✍ I Do Not Want to Go Back, Grandma. Please Let Me Stay!

> Three different times I begged the Lord to take it away. Each time he said, "My grace is all you need. My power works best in weakness." So now I am glad to boast about my weaknesses, so that the power of Christ can work through me. That's why I take pleasure in my weaknesses, and in the insults, hardships, persecutions, and troubles that I suffer for Christ. For when I am weak, then I am strong. (2 Corinthians 12:8–10 NLT)

Summer ended, and I had to go back to reality. Back to the war zone: Mom's crying and Dad's yelling. I took a piece of Grandma's peace with me and buried it deep down inside. When times got hard, I would go back to that place of peace, right next to my grandma.

When I got home, my mom got a crazy idea to move to this little Southern town in Texas where she had graduated from high school. Our house in Vegas was sold in a couple of days. Our things were packed, and we were on our way to my safe haven. Oh no, did Mom forget to do something? Oh yes, tell Dad and the courts that we were moving. Oops! Yes, Mom took me out of state without permission from the courts.

In this new small town, Mom bought a cool brick home with sweet tomato vines growing up the picket fence in the backyard. My room was decorated in turquoise and black. I started training for basketball tryouts. I got to go to my first dance. I wore a black, long, tight-fitting dress with my long brown hair perfectly curled and in place. I was very nervous, but the dance was exciting.

When I started school, I met a group of girls who did not care for me. I was a threat to their territory. There was one girl, though, Taylor, who was so kind and friendly. I did not know it then, but this nice girl would track me down wherever I went and would insist on not giving up on our friendship. She taught me the importance of loyalty. I was very thankful to have her in my life.

I remember having class with a group of loud, rowdy boys. They were very rude. They only had girls on the brain. One boy, who was quiet and kind, caught my attention when he would walk past my desk when the bell rang. I did not know it then but that nice, quiet boy would later break my heart.

While I was enjoying my new home and new school, my dad was not very happy about the move. He spent a lot of time and money in lawyer fees to get me back.

౬ **No, I Do Not Want to Live in the City!**

After I had been in school in my new town for about a month, Mom was court ordered to return to Vegas for a hearing. My mom felt she had nothing to worry about. She thought we would drive for twelve hours to Vegas. We would go to the court hearing, and then I would be coming back with her after the hearing. No big deal! So, I just had a few items packed. We went to the court hearing. I sat in a separate room in the courthouse, waiting to go back to my new home in Texas. My mom and dad went in to a big courtroom. My grandma and Aunt Molly came to support Mom; they sat in the courtroom to listen to the hearing. The big judge gave my dad custody. I could hear my mom screaming, "No!" loudly in the hallway. They forced her into an elevator, crying and yelling mean, angry words. Dad and his girlfriend came into the cold, quiet room I was waiting in. They told me the terrible news. I was heartbroken, shattered; I was unable to breathe. My nice little safe place was torn away from me. I remember going to my dad's house, straight to my new, dark room, and crying. I cried all night. I went into a very dark place inside. I closed myself off from the world. I buried my feelings deep down inside and decided I was not going to feel anything ever again. I prayed every night, "Please, God, bless me to go back, please!"

I spent my eighth-grade year in Vegas, closed off. I would not allow myself to have any joy, any fun. I wanted to be with my grandma. I hated the big city. I hated the big, crowded schools. I dreaded crazy traffic. I could not bear the miserable, dry, hot, desert heat and the stressful tension always in the air.

My dad did try. He knew I loved Sawyer Brown. He used his connections to get passes to meet the band before a concert. I remember waiting in a hotel conference room with a small group of people enjoying appetizers, anxiously waiting to meet the Traveling Band! I remember it like it was yesterday. Mark Miller was dressed in a faded army green polo shirt, and Gregg "Hobie" Hubbard walked in the room so casual. I had it all planned. I, fourteen years old, was going to tell Mark Miller how his voice was my safe zone. How I had played "Heart Don't Fall Now" over a hundred times. How I would escape into their music when things would get too hard. Their music was the place I found peace in this painful time in my life. When they walked up, two normal, down-to-earth guys, I froze, unable to speak. I just smiled, shook their hands, and took a picture; and then they were gone like a "Passing Train."

෩ This Battle Is Not Over; Keep on Fighting!

My mom fought the courts all year. She would drive twelve hours to come and see me every month. She brought her tears and hate with her each time. I did not want to be with her so much. I knew she was unstable. I wanted to be by my grandma and in a small town. During that year, I was assigned my own lawyer. He was supposed to look out for my best interests. I just remember his large, dark, hairy eyebrows and the way he made me feel nervous and scared. Something was wrong with this picture. This new, scary lawyer got the courts to grant my mom's sister, Aunt Molly, custody of me. I moved into their small townhouse.

My mom and dad were very upset about this new arrangement. Molly registered me at a scary, new middle school on the other side of town in Vegas. I unpacked my small amount of things in my new room that I would share with my cousin, Jane and tried to settle in.

Dad was very upset with the idea of me living with my Aunt Molly. Dad said he would allow me to go back to live with my mom if I would just come back to his house. I agreed to come back to his house with the understanding that Dad would help me get back to Texas. He had one of his employees build this large wooden crate to pack all my stuff in. I was so excited. I felt this large cloud of darkness leave. I packed all my things in this large heavy crate and waited. Days turned into weeks; weeks turned into months. Dad blamed the courts for not allowing me to go home. So, instead of going back to the small southern town, as I had hoped, I had to re-enroll in a school in the middle of the hot desert full of kids I did not allow myself to get close to.

ತ I Was Inspired in Art Class.

> As the light approaches, the earth takes
> shape like clay pressed beneath a seal; it is
> robed in brilliant colors. (Job 38:14 NLT)

Stuck in this place I did not want to be, I was inspired by an art teacher. He was a small older man with a small ponytail holding a tiny amount of gray hair touching his neck. I liked him. He challenged the creativity buried inside of me. One art assignment was to make your favorite sandwich out of clay. Well, my favorite sandwich was a croissant turkey breast with avocado, bacon, tomato, lettuce, cheese, and mayo. I believe I threw in some black olives too. Yes, I made it! My sandwich looked good enough to eat. Everything fit in its perfect place. I used watercolors to paint each piece to look real. That sandwich sure sounds good right now.

ತ Yes! I Get to Go Back to My Safe Haven!

> What's more, I am with you, and I will
> protect you wherever you go. One day I
> will bring you back to this land. I will not
> leave you until I have finished giving you
> everything I have promised you. (Genesis
> 28:15 NLT)

Even though Mom was still unstable, my dad loved me enough to let me go where my heart was. It was in this small, little town close to my grandma where the summers were filled with old green trees, bugs, and grandma telling stories as we drank our coffee with milk and sugar! I was finally granted permission to go back. Yes! The cloud was lifted, or was it? I flew back and forth from my mom's to my dad's once a month to see my dad. My parents were still in court, battling out who had more anger.

> He tells us everything over and over—one line at a time, one line at a time, a little here, and a little there!" So now God will have to speak to his people through foreign oppressors who speak a strange language! God has told his people, "Here is a place of rest; let the weary rest here. This is a place of quiet rest." But they would not listen. So the Lord will spell out his message for them again, one line at a time, one line at a time, a little here, and a little there, so that they will stumble and fall. They will be injured, trapped, and captured. (Isaiah 28:10–13 NLT)

Things were good. I had my grandma and my small town. I started ninth grade, a freshman in my mom's old high school. I was nervous. I remember having algebra; they tried a new method in our class. We were taught algebra using these turquoise and purple blocks: long ones, medium ones, and short ones. It felt like we spent half the year learning how to use the blocks instead of learning algebra. I thought French sounded cool, so I signed up for a French class. My new French teacher was short and stout. She had red hair cut in a bob. She wore glasses. She spoke very good French. I found out quickly that my gift was not foreign languages, especially not speaking them. I took advantage of every extra credit project she offered. It was Christmas time, and she said we could make a Christmas poster with a Christmas greeting written in French. Well, I copied the spelling of one of the displayed posters hanging up. I worked very hard during the weekend on my poster that read "Feliz Navidad!" When she saw it, she looked at me, shook her head, and just rolled her eyes. Who knew a French teacher could also teach Spanish. I will never forget that "Feliz Navidad" means Merry Christmas in Spanish!

Remember that group of girls who felt I was intruding in their territory? They thought they would teach me a lesson. While I was in P.E. class, my 49ers jacket and 8-ball shirt were stolen. I had to wear my P.E. shirt the rest of the day. It was okay; they could have my old 49ers jacket! I got an awesome new 49ers jacket that the coaches wore on the sidelines during the football games. Here I was in Cowboys territory, and I was a 49ers fan. I sure liked to cause conflict! I loved to watch Jerry Rice. I would get goosebumps when the ball flew high in the sky and then fell perfectly into Jerry Rice's hands. Touch down! Yeah! Mom bought me all kinds of Jerry Rice stuff: shirts, bobblehead dolls, cups, plaques, plates, jerseys, and football cards. I had a room that just displayed 49ers stuff. Yeah, I know, a little bit much. My mom was like that. I would find an interest, and she would go overboard. I mentioned something about thinking this one picture of a fish was cool. When I came home from a visit with my dad, my whole bedroom and bathroom were done in fish. I had fish on the walls; I had little wooden fish accessories and fish on my bed. It was very fishy.

ೞ **Mom, I am Growing Up!**

> Don't be concerned about the outward beauty of fancy hairstyles, expensive jewelry, or beautiful clothes. You should clothe yourselves instead with the beauty that comes from within, the unfading beauty of a gentle and quiet spirit, which is so precious to God. (1 Peter 3:3–4 NLT)

Something happened to that little chubby girl. She stretched out and got a little confidence. I still was not happy with my appearance, especially my legs. I never liked my legs. I liked to wear short skirts with tights, fitted shirts, and blue jeans. My hair was golden brown, just past my shoulders. I would get up early every morning to curl my hair, trying to make it perfect. One girl accused me, in the middle of class, of wearing a wig! No, it was my real hair; I just had a perfection problem.

I found that nice girl Taylor. We became good friends. And that boy—where did he go? Well, he was around at lunchtime! We would have to go outside after lunch and kind of wait around until the bell rang. I was almost fifteen years old, and I had the biggest crush on him. He played all sports. He was very strong for a freshman. I got brave one day and put words to a song sung by Tevin Campbell in his back pocket as we were walking in from lunch. We started to go out not long after I gave him that note. Going out—what did that mean? He would walk me to my classes. We would talk on the phone after school. I did not like to call him. I did not want to bother him or seem needy. I went to all of his football and baseball games, and we would go to school dances together. I remember one dance where we were supposed to dress like twins. I wore a red shirt with suspenders holding up my short black skirt. I bought him a red shirt and suspenders too. He wore his red shirt with a pair of blue jeans. He thought I was crazy, but we had fun. Oh, first loves!

During that time, my mom was still depressed. She would lay in her room and cry all day. She was still not too motivated to get out of her pajamas. Mom was filled with intense anger deep inside. She would attack Dad using lawyers, and he would reply with anger. It was still very stressful for me.

I was unable to control the stress or my menstrual cycle. I would hemorrhage for weeks. I was embarrassed to go to school, afraid of soiling my clothes. It overtook my life. One day, in sixth period, I bled through my pants onto a white chair. Praying that no one noticed, I acted as if nothing was wrong, put my jacket down low, and walked out of class. My mom picked me up that day. I started crying. I told her I was not going back to school until I was fixed. She took me to the doctor the next day. They took more blood for testing. Sure, take more blood! As I was standing, waiting for Mom to finish paperwork in the doctor's office, I remember falling straight back onto the hard floor. I had passed out. The next thing I remember was being pushed in a wheelchair outside toward the hospital close by. I had to spend the night in the hospital and watch two bags of blood get pumped back into me.

I had two visitors during my stay in the hospital: Taylor and the young man who held my heart. He gave me his school picture. On the back of it, he wrote, "I love you". Did he love me? What part of me did he love? The part of me that wanted to stand out, who did not want to be the same as everyone else? Did he love the depressed part of me trying to bring him down or the silly one who tried to make her friends laugh? Or did he love the part of me that would not allow anyone to know she was afraid of getting hurt, hidden behind the tough girl image? Did he love the part of me who would not eat lunch at school because she did not want to be judged for what she ate or called a fat pig? Did he love the girl who would cry and pray at night for the nightmare she was in to end as she listened to Sawyer Brown's "Passing Train" over and over again? Did he love her? No, because I would not allow anyone to see that person, that weak, confused, unhappy person. We went out for most of ninth grade. That summer, he went away to work. He never told me he was leaving. I heard it from his cousin one night at an arcade hangout. I acted like it did not hurt me, but it did. I thought I was supposed to be this strong girl who did not care, but I did care. He broke my heart.

I thought it was going to be perfect in my new southern town. I had worked so hard to get there. Although I had a good ninth grade year, a tornado was coming! I was to meet some people that summer who would change my life. More challenges were on their way!

ເ◌ Sometimes We Think the Grass Is Greener on the Other Side!

My mom and grandma rented this building on Main Street. They turned it into a cute store full of pictures, accents, and antiques to decorate homes. My mom was good at decorating; she would spend hours creating flower arrangements with ribbons and bows. She would glue birds in the arrangement or make an arrangement using antique silverware. She would create new ways to use old windows, shelves, chairs, or doors. Mom's gifts were in decorating, not money. My grandma took care of the bills. My mom, not being able to understand the difference between a lie and the truth, caused conflict. Mom still had the "everyone owes me" monster inside. She would take money from the store and lie about it; she would make promises to customers and then break them. Well, she met her match one day when a woman came in.

She had the same challenges as Mom. This lady had two daughters. One girl, Nikki, was a year older than me in school. She was in beauty pageants, and Mom thought I needed to hang around her so I could be in pageants and become popular. Mom was popular in school; she thought I should be too, so she really pushed the friendship. My mom entered me in local beauty pageants and encouraged me to go do things with Nikki. This caused conflict in my relationship with Taylor. Taylor knew Nikki and her ability to manipulate. Taylor pushed away from me. I spent the rest of my summer hanging out with Nikki, knowing I could not trust her.

My mom and dad were still battling it out in court. One day I walked home from school, and my mother wasn't there. Her car was at the house, but she was not. I got worried and called my grandma. I came to find out my mom had been arrested for something. I did not understand why, but I was sure my dad was involved. I remember going to the small-town sheriff's office and seeing my mom. She pulled me aside and asked me to lie to the sheriff. She wanted me to say Dad had been hurting me. I yelled at her and said I was not going to say that; it was not true. I am not sure why, but Mom went to the county jail for a couple months.

While Mom was still in jail, I went to the back-to-school dance with Nikki. We both were broken-hearted over our old boyfriends. We decided to go as two single girls. The plan was to have fun without boyfriends. Yeah, right! She changed those plans. As we walked into the dance, this guy yelled at me, "Hey, sexy!" No one had ever said that to me before. Miss Insecure took it as a compliment.

At the dance that night, a boy who I was scared of asked me to dance. I said, "Sorry, I'm dancing with him." And I turned around, and there was the boy from the parking lot who had yelled at me. As I danced with him for a while,

Nikki was making up with her boyfriend. I did not know that this boy was good friends with Nikki's boyfriend. Nikki left the dance with her boyfriend and had planned for me to ride home with this boy I did not know. Well, he thought he would go show me the stars. I thought the stars he was talking about were in the sky. I rejected his stars, and he said no one had ever turned him down before. He said he respected me. Later he would say he believed he fell in love with me that night. Yeah, right! Well, his name was Matt. He started coming around often. I was still broken-hearted but liked the attention. He was a senior, and I was a sophomore.

While my mom was still in jail, my grandma and Aunt Molly would take turns staying with me at my house. Mr. Matt, a wild party animal, would knock on my window at midnight. I would get up, open the back door, and watch him puke in my backyard. This would be the start of a bad pattern. He would go to parties, get drunk, and then come knocking on my door every Friday night. I would watch him throw up into the dark night. I was uncomfortable with this disgusting ritual. I was a good girl and did not drink or party. I was not sure what to do with him. My mom finally came home from jail. She connected with Matt and took him in as a lost son, promising him the world. I just rolled my eyes.

One day I got brave and went to a football game to watch the one who still had my heart. I was trying to wait and talk to him after the game, but my mom drove up in one of her rages, yelling at me to get in the car. I was so embarrassed. We never did talk face-to-face again.

Matt kept hanging around. I think he liked the attention from my mother. He did not have much; he wore hand-me-down girl jeans and worn-out shoes. My mom went out and bought him new pants, shirts, and shoes. At night, they would talk and dream about the money that Mom was going to get from suing my dad. She promised to buy him all kinds of things. They were both in a material dream world. I would get upset and tell Mom she needed to let go of the hate and move on.

Mom's lawyer came up with a way for this custody battle to end. I could hear the angels blowing their horns, singing, "Hallelujah!" The solution was to marry me off for thirty days, and then I would become an adult. Mom promised Matt that as long as he was married to me, he would be taken care of. Well, Matt, who had just turned nineteen, agreed to marry me. I had only been sixteen for thirty days. Matt told me if he married me, it would be forever and not just for thirty days. I agreed to his deal. I was so desperate to end the eight-year World War III custody nightmare. This was my ticket out of the hate and anger of both my parents. We were married on a dark night in January. A local pastor agreed to marry us in my mother's home. I wore a navy blue sailor dress. He wore a pair of everyday jeans and a T-shirt. My mom and Aunt Molly were both there. We went to a local steakhouse for dinner after we said, "I do." It was not my ideal wedding, but life up to that point had not been so ideal either.

The pastor who married us that night was also a substitute teacher. He knew about Matt being wild and wanted to make an example out of him. He invited Matt and me to church and activities. Matt liked the attention. I was uncomfortable and felt like I did not fit in. All the women wore dresses and had long hair; I always wore jeans and had just cut off my long hair. They shared information about the beast of the book of Revelation being in the television and in debit cards. This scared me. I did not want to watch TV anymore, and debit cards were just coming out. This caused conflict with Matt and me. He did not take the information on the beast literally, but I did.

Matt graduated from high school that year. I remember driving home with Matt one day. He was talking about our future. He informed me that I would have to lose weight. He was not going to be married to a fat woman. I believe I gained a pound each day from that moment on. Here was this man who was supposed to be my partner, telling me, Miss Already Self-Conscious—who has struggled with weight forever knowing that her dad hates fat women—that I needed to lose more weight. I was already at my best weight! This made me push away and close off from him.

ஒ Impressed by Money!

My dad was angry with the situation but was trying to restore a relationship with me. The summer after Matt graduated, my dad invited us out to his home in Vegas. He flew his personal airplane to Texas to meet us. Here this short, Irish man gets out of the plane. With this serious look on his face, Dad looked at Matt—six feet, three inches tall—straight in the eyes, firmly shook his hand, and said, "I do not like you, but I will learn to love you." As we flew over the Grand Canyon, Matt got sick. Later, talking about getting sick in the airplane, Matt called the Grand Canyon a creek! That was funny!

Matt was so impressed by Dad's money and lifestyle. After seeing everything Dad had, and all the promises he made, Matt wanted to move to Vegas. We had been married for about six months. Matt worked for my dad's construction company. He delivered fuel and parts to the cranes all around town.

Before we left Texas, the place I fought so hard for, we bought a black Lab named Mozy. We moved into Dad's motor home on some land he owned, next to his house. Dad's third wife, the nice Italian woman, had bought some fancy chickens. They produced pretty, colored eggs. Our new lab, Mozy, ate the fancy chickens. Matt heard that you are supposed to tie a dead chicken around the dog's neck and let the chicken decay. The smell of the rotten chicken was supposed to break Mozy of eating chickens. So he tried it. It did not work. She repaid us by pooping on our marriage license while left alone in the motor home. I guess she showed us!

I was eager to graduate, but I did not want to go back to high school and be the weird, married girl. I looked for other ways to graduate. As I was looking into homeschooling, Matt's friend, Nikki's boyfriend, was in the city doing construction work for his dad. This was not good. Chip and Matt were old buddies from high school who liked to drink and get into trouble. This caused conflict. Matt started to get homesick and tired of my dad's tough lessons. Chip found out his seventeen-year-old girlfriend, Nikki, was pregnant back home. Chip and Matt came up with a plan to move to the Panhandle, ninety miles away from Matt's hometown, and work for Chip's cousin. Well, that did not go over well with Dad. He told Matt he would never make something of himself. He gave us $1,500, and we were on our way. I was scared but believed I was supposed to follow my husband.

On the way back to the Panhandle, each in our own car, Chip bailed on us. When we arrived in this new small town, Chip was nowhere to be found. That job he promised Matt did not exist. So we found a one-room apartment, budgeted our money, and tried to figure out what to do next. Matt went and applied at this big pig-slaughtering plant and was hired two weeks later. While waiting for the job, we hung out in our small, one-room shack.

My mom came up and tried to help decorate this small space. I was inspired to sponge paint the kitchen wall red and blue. Well, you know red and blue make purple. It is true; I proved it! The landlord came by one day. He was not too happy about my paint job. He still offered to rent us an old, small, white house that he had fixed up. It was nice and clean. It had a big kitchen, a nice front room, and one bedroom. It was just perfect for us. After living in the shack for three weeks, we moved into this nice clean home in a safer neighborhood.

Matt started work during second shift at the local pig plant on the conveyer line, cutting some part of the pig. He would wake up in the middle of the night with aching pains in his hands. He was told to soak his hands in Epsom salt. He got tired of his hands aching, so he applied to be a third-shift maintenance man. He got the job and seemed to like it.

While he was working, I was searching for a way to graduate. I went to the library to find out information about homeschooling. I asked the librarian for help. She gave me the name of a woman who homeschooled her family in town. I took the number and called her right away on a pay phone outside. She invited me over to her house and showed me information on the homeschooling curriculum she used with her family. It was a Christian curriculum. I took the information, went straight home, and signed up for homeschooling. At sixteen years old, I applied for a job at the local discount store. They told me that they normally do not hire under the age of eighteen but decided to take a chance on me. During my lunch breaks, I would do my schoolwork.

I worked in the health and beauty aids department. I was in charge of keeping this area stocked, clean, and straightened up. I took my job very seriously. I was a hard worker. There was this other girl in health and beauty aids during the evening shift. She was a college student from the Rockies. She was not as focused as I was, nor did she take her job seriously. She would not get her work finished at night, which meant I would have to do her work the next day before I could complete my list. This caused me frustration. I allowed myself to be overworked and burnt out. That hemorrhaging problem that I had would come around when I was stressed and take over. I quit working at the local discount store only to find out that they were about to transfer me to my own department and make me department manager of housewares. That made me sick; my problem would have been solved if I had stuck in there. My pattern was to run away. This was not a good pattern! I wish I had known the following scripture!

> So do not throw away this confident trust
> in the Lord. Remember the great reward
> it brings you! Patient endurance is what
> you need now, so that you will continue
> to do God's will. Then you will receive all
> that he has promised. (Hebrews 10:35–
> 36 NLT)

Now without a job to worry about, I focused hard on my studies and graduated a year early as an honor student. I was able to walk across the stage to receive my diploma. Before the graduation ceremony, we had to go to this parents' information meeting. Guess who I sat next to? Yes, the woman who, a year prior, had given me the information about homeschooling. Her daughter was graduating too. She was shocked to see me there. Oh, how we live in a circle! My mom and Matt were the only ones who came to my graduation. My dad did not come because of my mother. I was hoping that he had quietly come and was sitting up in the balcony, but he was not. We stayed in a motel and went out to eat that night. It was nice, but I was disappointed that no one else had come. My grandma, my aunts, my cousins—none of them came. It was just us. Well, I did it. I was determined to graduate, and I did. Now on to other challenges.

❧ A Marriage without a Blessing.

My marriage to Matt had always been a challenge. We always argued. He was still going out every once in a while and getting drunk. I did not like or trust him when he went out. He was very good at turning things around and blaming me. I struggled with trusting and opening up to him. I wanted intimacy and romance. He said it did not exist. I just pushed away from him even more.

> Give justice to the poor and the orphan; uphold the rights of the oppressed and the destitute. Rescue the poor and helpless; deliver them from the grasp of evil people. But these oppressors know nothing; they are so ignorant! They wander about in darkness, while the whole world is shaken to the core. (Psalm 82:3–5 NLT)

What kind of life had Matt had? It had not been a very stable childhood. His mother suffered from being abandoned by her mother. Her father had not been a stable figure either. Matt's father had served in the military. He enjoyed women. He took his flirting too far too many times. Matt's mom and dad married and had three boys. Matt was the middle child. It was not long after Matt's younger brother was born that his parents divorced. Matt's parents also battled in court for custody. I believe not being in a loving family growing up, Matt's mom did not know how to be compassionate toward her boys. She allowed a drug addict to come into her family's home. Matt and his two brothers were raised around people doing drugs, drinking, and engaging in other negative activities. This definitely affected Matt emotionally.

These three brothers grew up wild. They were active in stealing, dealing drugs, and drinking alcohol. Matt's older brother ended up in prison for drugs. Matt dealt drugs in high school. He was sexually active at a young age. I did not know all this until after we were married. Boy, was I naive! Matt's younger brother followed in his older brother's footsteps. He added getting a very young girl pregnant to the list. Matt seemed determined not to be a failure. He was the only one in his family to graduate from high school. I believe he pushed at being a success to prove to himself he was not a disappointment. However, the negatives from his past haunted him in his future. He was unable to communicate these feelings and ended up following in his mother's footsteps by hiding his pain in alcohol.

ಟಿ **Dad is Coming to Visit!**

My dad decided to come and check on us. He flew in his personal airplane with his pilot and a new girlfriend. This was a shock to me. I didn't know that he was not with the nice Italian woman anymore. Dad's new girlfriend was nice. Dad said he was proud of us. He liked the house we were renting. He was impressed that we had not wasted the $1,500 he had given us when we decided to move. We were doing well, so Dad found a realtor to show us houses for sale that same day. Matt was at work and did not know what was going on. Dad found a house he thought was a good buy and made an offer on the house that same day. The offer was accepted. Dad wrote a check for $15,000 to use as a down payment. Then he left that same night. Wow, that was a visit. Matt called to check in that night. I told him I was moving and he could come if he wanted. He got nervous. He did not know what was going on. Here I was, seventeen years old and a new homeowner. Within thirty days, we were moved into our new three-bedroom home in our small town in the Panhandle. It had a nice fenced-in backyard, a cute kitchen, one bathroom, and a nice living room. My mom came up and helped decorate the house. We painted the front room a perfect cherry red, and painted the baseboards and trim white. Mom found a beautiful border with old cottage houses accented in reds, yellows, and blues to hang in the front room. I loved that border. We put new marble-white carpet throughout the house. Wow, three places in one year! We were busy bees!

๛ Mom, What Are You up To?

What was Mom doing now? Grandma and Mom closed down their cute, little store. Grandma moved back to Vegas to be near Aunt Molly. Mom found a big, two-story yellow house to rent. She turned it into a store and a place for tea parties, a place the local ladies could play cards and have lunch. She seemed to be doing well. Then out of the blue, she met this older man and was quickly married. Do not ask me why! This marriage would be over quickly too!

You would think things would be going great for me. I was married and out from the middle of a custody battle. Now, I was finally in control of my own life. No, the grass was not so green on the other side of the fence! I tried to act as if it was okay, but it was not. Matt and I still argued; he found a group of friends to party and drink with. It made me feel uncomfortable. I wrote a letter to my friend Taylor. I expressed my frustrations about the marriage and how I missed the boy who still had my heart. She shared the letter with him. I got a phone call one day; it was him. The first boy to say he loved me—the first boy to give me butterflies in my stomach when I heard his voice. We talked about the past and the gossip that kept us apart. He knew about the lawyer's idea to marry me off to Matt. I was praying to God while I was on the phone with him, knowing it was wrong to have feelings for him. He said something that made me realize he was still a boy and that I had changed. Our priorities were different. He was still a child in high school, and I had no choice. I had to grow up and act like an adult.

But, against my better judgment I agreed to meet him on a dirt road halfway between our homes on a certain day. Knowing it was wrong, I prayed for something to happen so I couldn't go. Well, my mom came to spend the night before I was supposed to meet him; then a snowstorm came the next day. My mom got up very early and left to go back home. She said she could hear mice and had to leave. On her way home in the snowstorm, she was hit head-on by a school bus. Well, I would say that was something that "happened." I never went to meet him, and we would never talk again.

> The temptations in your life are no different
> from what others experience. And God is
> faithful. He will not allow the temptation
> to be more than you can stand. When you
> are tempted, he will show you a way out
> so that you can endure. (1 Corinthians
> 10:13 NLT)

Is that what God did? Provide a way out? I felt guilty for what happened to Mom. I thought my sin had caused her accident.

৪৩ No, I Am Not Pregnant!

On top of everything else, I had a health problem too. I went to the doctor's office because I had not had a period in three months. Even though I did not mind not bleeding, I thought I should check it out. They did a pregnancy test, and it came back negative. I remember sitting in the hallway feeling disappointed. A month later, I was supposed to come back for more tests. They took me into this room. I changed into one of those wonderful cotton gowns, with the snaps in the back, and climbed up on the examining table, trying to stay on the paper. I waited for the doctor. The doctor wanted to see if my uterus was okay, so he used an ultrasound to see what was going on inside. There was this nurse in the room during the ultrasound. I remember her falling back against the door in shock and gasping for air. It scared me. I thought there was something terribly wrong inside me. Perhaps something was missing or in the wrong place. No, nothing was wrong. I was only three months pregnant with my first baby. What, me pregnant? Just a couple weeks ago I had failed the test, and now they said this little gift was growing inside of me. What?

Well, I called and left a message for Matt on our home answering machine to bring our checkbook to the doctor's office. I met him in the parking lot. He rolled down the car window to hand me the checkbook, and I told him the news. We both cried with excitement. Something changed that day. I was not just living for myself anymore. I was going to be a mom! When we got home, we called everyone with the news. Matt called my dad. He was not talking to me at that time. We had had an argument on the phone. Mom had attacked Dad with some kind of scheme, and he wanted me to disown her. I told him that I did not want to be in the middle of their war anymore. That is why I had gotten married. He did not like my answer and disowned me. Matt was upset with him on the phone and said I was his daughter-that I was having his first grandchild and to let it go. Dad's heart was still hard. I did not talk to him for the next nine months.

During my pregnancy, I wondered how my biological mom felt when she was pregnant with me. Here I was, eighteen years old, about the same age as my biological mom when she was pregnant with me. I thought about what it would feel like to carry a child inside, feel her move and grow. I wondered how she felt when she carried me. Did she become numb to me inside her, knowing she was going to give me up? Did she hate me for growing inside of her? Or, did her heart break each time I moved, knowing that she would never see me grow up? As I have grown up, I have been thankful that she gave me up instead of having an abortion. I try to believe that God has a purpose for me and that I was not unwanted or a mistake.

> "For I know the plans I have for you," says the Lord. "They are plans for good and not for disaster, to give you a future and a hope. 12 In those days when you pray, I will listen. 13 If you look for me wholeheartedly, you will find me. (Jeremiah 29:11–13 NLT)

My mom, who could not have children, tried to live through my pregnancy.

My First Baby Was Born!

We never found out the gender of our baby during our pregnancy. I was so thankful when the doctor said, "It's a girl!" A beautiful baby girl, named Brooke, was born three weeks early. I had prayed so hard for a baby girl who looked just like me. Being adopted, I missed out on seeing where my eyes and my personality came from and who I looked like the most. I would always study families and see who looked like who. The Lord blessed me with a healthy baby girl who would grow up looking like my twin. We even have the same personality. We are both sensitive, and when we get hurt, we try to hold it all in. Boy, raising her, I see how dramatic I was! Brook has grown up to become a very beautiful young lady. I have tried to tell her each day how special she is, trying to build her up so she can fight those mean insecurities that attack.

What Do You Do with Mother?

Mom's leg was crushed in the head-on collision with the bus. She was restricted to a wheelchair. In surgery, they put in steel rods to hold her ankle in place. She stayed with her husband for a while. After having a breakdown and threatening to kill herself, she came and lived with Matt and me. Her short-term husband filed for divorce. She was unable to run her store and lost her business and the yellow house. We packed all of Mom's clothes, furniture, and extra baggage she had been carrying for too long and moved her in with us. She called around to find a place to store her belongings. A Lutheran Church pastor agreed to store all her things in a room at the church.

This pastor started coming around and visiting with Mom. He did not look like your typical pastor. He wore camel pants, T-shirts, and flip-flops. He drove an old, brown, rusty van. He was very relaxed and easy to talk to. I would listen in as I held my newborn baby girl on my lap. I started asking questions about the beast in the television and debit cards. He laughed at me and started to explain Jesus to me. This was the first time in my life that someone explained to me the importance of Jesus Christ and how much He loves me.

My mom had me baptized in a Lutheran Church as an infant. As I grew up, I went to Sunday School at a Mormon Church. I was baptized in the Mormon Church at the age of eight. The only thing I really remember about Sunday School is a song we used to sing. My mom had my name painted in watercolor with the words "I am a child of God, and He has sent me here, has given me an earthly home with parents kind and dear, lead me, guide me, walk beside me, help me find the way. Teach me all that I must know, to live with Him someday!" I used to sing these words to help me fall asleep or when I was worried. Being adopted, these words made me feel like I was not a mistake and I did have a purpose. Growing up, I did not know much about God, but I knew that I desperately needed His help.

Matt and I started to go to church. We completed an adult confirmation class at the pastor's church and became confirmed Lutherans.

Shortly after we were confirmed, Mom got her settlement from the accident. During this whole process, Mom was causing many problems at home between Matt and me. She would always dwell on how she was the victim. How everyone had abused her. How she deserved half of everything Dad had. How she was abused as a child and how she did not understand why I did not love her enough. She would call her friends, her sisters, and her mom. She would tell them how I was abusing her. This broke my heart. Here I was, opening up my home to her, and she was backstabbing me. I would get upset and yell at her, "You have to let it go! You have to move on with your life." She could not let go of the hate and anger. I did not like who I was when I was around her. I would become filled with this anger and frustration. It was not healthy for my daughter, Brooke, to hear all this fighting. When Mom's settlement came, we sold our house to her and moved to Vegas to live with my dad. You see, my marriage to Matt did not solve any problems. It just added to the pile. I was still a ping-pong ball running from parent to parent. This time I was the parent of a six month old.

We loaded up a U-Haul truck with all of our personal things. Matt, a six-month-old baby, and I headed back to the place I tried so hard to get away from-for the third time! They say the third time is a charm! Was it going to be? Dad said we could live with him while we built a house next door on the same property we had stayed on in a motor home two years before. Do you remember Mozy, the chickens and the soiled marriage license? This same property had a garage with a bathroom already built and a brick wall surrounding the property with a little gate one could use to go to Dad's house. Dad had created a structural steel erection company as well as his crane company over the years. He told Matt if he worked hard, he could take over the company in a couple of years. All Matt could hear was money and power. He was not concerned about anything else. I was not too sure about it. I was raised in this business. I knew it would take everything he had, not leaving any time for our family.

> Wherever your treasure is, there the
> desires of your heart will also be.
> (Matthew 6:21 NLT)

He wanted the money and the power; he wanted it all, no matter what the cost.

So we lived with Dad and his new fiancée. Matt worked long hours trying to learn everything Dad knew about the steel business. I was at Dad's house taking care of Brooke. I was not too happy with the situation. When you make deals with my dad, there are always stipulations. If we built this house, my mom, my grandma, or Aunt Molly's family would never be allowed to come over. That bothered me, but I felt I did not have any choice. You see, years prior my dad and his Italian girlfriend stayed in the motor home at the office, and some men dressed up as black ninjas came and robbed him two nights in a row.

The men who were caught knew my cousin's husband. Dad felt that his life was in danger and that Mom had hired them to kill him. He did not want any of my mom's family around his property!

✂ Money and Power, or Family: Can You Have Both?

My husband was so focused on being this powerful businessman he did not have time for his family. He definitely did not consider our feelings. He claimed that he was doing all this for us. He was not; he was doing it to prove to himself that he was not a failure. Matt played my dad and me. He would lie and manipulate situations to benefit himself. He would complain to Dad about me. He would complain to me about Dad. I was struggling with living in my dad's house again with my husband, who I feared was going to turn into my dad-an angry, power-driven man who was stressed out because of business. It was hard for Dad to let go and relax with his family. I did not want my children growing up in the same stressful atmosphere I did.

One day, Dad came home early from work. He sat down in a wooden chair in the living room, and I sat on the couch, staring at him with Brooke playing on the floor. Dad said he had been watching me and was concerned about my behavior toward my husband. He began to tear me down. He told me if I did not straighten up my act, I would be in a mental institution like my mom or become a divorced, single mom on welfare. I remember Dad's girlfriend sitting in the kitchen. I was hoping she would step in and tell him to stop, but she didn't. She just stared at me. He made me feel that an unstable marriage full of lies and emotional abuse was better than being divorced. He did not know what was going on. I thought you were not supposed to tell anyone your problems, fearing they would judge Matt. I just sat there trying to hold in my tears, unable to catch my breath from stifled crying. That father figure you are supposed to trust and look up to was tearing me down to where I felt worthless, not worthy of being a mom or wife. After his lecture, I was supposed to put myself together. We went out to dinner that night. I was supposed to act as if nothing was wrong. Here I was again, pretending that everything was okay, but dying inside. When I got home that night, I went to that same cold room that I had cried in years before when the court forced me to live with Dad. I felt so worthless. I believed my daughter would be better off if I was dead. I knew where Dad kept the gun in his bedroom. I was going to kill myself the next day while everyone was at work. A small voice inside stopped me. It said if I killed myself, then I would not be able to meet Jesus. That was the only thing that stopped me, the desire to meet Jesus in heaven.

I closed myself off from my dad and Matt even more. I turned my focus on becoming the best mom I could be. I became very active in a local Lutheran Church. I helped with a mom's group twice a month and worked on the nursery committee. My life changed when I became the chairperson of fellowship at church.

> God has given each of you a gift from
> his great variety of spiritual gifts. Use
> them well to serve one another. (1 Peter
> 4:10 NLT)

❧ I Found a Way to Use My Gifts!

I found joy in something I was good at. I created activities
and planned dinners. My creativity came out. I started to
feel important. Matt would come to church and act as if he
was following Jesus, but then Monday came and his focus
changed. I took it seriously. I wanted to learn everything
I could. I wanted to build that relationship with Christ.
We both liked the pastor and his wife. They had adopted
two girls and liked to share their adoption story. The
pastor and his wife had moved from the Rockies. They
really loved the Rockies and only had good things to share
about their time there. Did you notice? This is the second
time the Rockies were brought up in my life. I started to
become interested in the Rockies. The girl I mentioned
who worked in the health and beauty aids at the local
discount store was from the Rockies, and now the pastor
was from there and just loved it.

I became good friends with Sarah; she was a member
of the same church. Her family had transferred from
Indiana to open a home improvement store. They always
had intentions of going back to Indiana. She had a little
girl a year older than Brooke. We would have play dates,
go shopping, and talk on the phone. I am very thankful

God brought her into my life. I really needed her. Life at home was not good.

೮ು Where Did Mom Go?

Mom sold the house she bought from us and moved to Oregon to live near her sister Ruth. She bought a small house in the same small town as her sister. Ruth's husband, Tim, agreed to restore Mom's house for her. It was completely stripped down and needed a new bathroom, new kitchen, wood flooring, new siding, and a new roof. Tim, who had not completed his own house, started to work on Mom's house. His progress was very slow; being a retired firefighter with health issues, he took his time.

Mom cannot live with someone for a long period of time without causing conflict. She followed her same pattern- always the victim. Ruth felt sorry for her at first. She cried to Ruth, saying I was a bad daughter who abused her and took advantage of her. I was just a horrible person in her eyes. Ruth believed Mom at first. She felt sorry for her. Well, Ruth's opinion started to change. She started to catch Mom in lies. She began to get frustrated with Mom's negative attitude and how she was unable to let go of the past.

I came and visited a month before Brooke's first birthday. It was a quaint, small town. Beautiful mountains full of trees surrounded the old lumber town. Ruth's house was a beautiful old Victorian house with three levels, wood flooring, beautiful wood trim, and tan paint with burgundy and hunter green accents. Mom's little house did have potential. Mom had no appreciation for Tim's hard work, only negative remarks: "He is wasting my money; he is too slow; he is doing it wrong."

I really enjoyed my visit with Aunt Ruth. This was the first time in many years that I had gotten to spend time with her. When I was an infant, Aunt Ruth was the aunt who turned my parents in to the Department of Human Services. So, for too many years, my mom and Ruth did not talk. I enjoyed the time we spent together. She was a great craft painter with such patience; she showed me how to do some different paint strokes. We talked about our sewing projects. I will treasure that special time forever.

I do have to stop and share a couple funny stories about Ruth's daughter, Emma. I was about seven, so Emma would have been about six years old. I was at my Aunt Molly's house the same time Emma was there. Emma really upset my other cousin, Jane, so badly that she put her inside a green, turtle shaped sandbox and sat on top of it. Can you believe that we both got in trouble! I was not strong enough to pick her up, and I would definitely not put someone in a sandbox-that would be too dirty! A couple of years later, when I was about thirteen years old, Emma and I walked to a local grocery store in Vegas to buy some ice cream. Emma, who seemed to be allergic to everything, wanted me to buy her something she could not eat. I told her no. She began to have a fake asthma attack in the checkout line. I was so embarrassed! When we got out of the store, I yelled at her and told her how much she had embarrassed me. When we were almost to her house, she spit on my feet and ran into her house. I was wearing sandals! I still remember the yucky feeling of warm spit in between my toes, sliding around in my sandals. I just went and sat in my mom's car and waited. I just knew that somehow I would get in trouble! Okay, so back to my visit with Mom!

It was a very nice visit, minus all of Mom's hateful words. She could not help but bring up that we moved to Dad's to hurt her. That we chose to live by my dad's rules and ripped Brooke away from her. I was just a horrible daughter.

ᘓ My Chance to See if I Have Talent Like Mom!

It was fun building my new house, creating and decorating it from the ground up, but was it worth it? Was it worth the stipulations? Was it worth being controlled? We chose to build a two thousand-square-foot, ranch-style house. It was a four-bedroom house with a large master bedroom and bathroom. It had a large open kitchen with lots of oak cabinets looking into a family room with a gas fireplace. It had a living and dining room separated by a half wall. I chose the popular cream colored paint with white trim. The master bedroom and bathroom were a green color accented with big cabbage roses and plaids. Brooke's room was a light pink. Remember Taylor? She became Brooke's godmother. She tried very hard to be involved in Brooke's life. She would send Brooke letters, books, and gifts. She came to visit and painted cute bunnies at the bottom of the walls in Brooke's room. They looked so real. I stenciled wild flowers around the bunnies. The bunnies looked like they were hiding in wild flowers. It turned out to be so cute. It took a year to build the house, and we lived in the house for a year.

∞ Did We Move by Faith?

Dad started acting funny. He had been to a doctor's appointment. The doctor told him his stressful lifestyle was killing him. The doctor said he did not have much time left to live. Dad did not feel Matt was ready to take over the company, so Dad decided to close down his crane and steel company. He allowed Matt to take all the welding equipment he needed to start his own steel erection company. Dad gave Matt a $20,000 check, a welding truck, welders, ladders, a welding rod, lead rope, and all kinds of tools. All Matt needed now was a business plan … and discipline. Dad auctioned off the rest of the welding equipment and his cranes and trucks. Matt was trying to figure out what he wanted to do. He decided he did not want to live in Vegas anymore. My mom said we should come and live by her. Matt made a quick trip to see if he liked it in this small town in a forest landscape. They looked at some houses. Matt was concerned about being able to make a living in the small town. This made Mom mad. She wanted us to move up there. I did not want to have to choose between parents again. I remember we were in the car, talking about where we were going to move. We were driving home, and Matt asked me where I wanted to move to. I did not answer him, but deep down inside I felt the desire to go to the Rockies. I prayed about it for a couple days.

> You are my rock and my fortress. For the honor of your name, lead me out of this danger. (Psalms 31:3 NLT)

I was struggling with the thought of leaving my new friends and my fellowship commitments at church. One morning I woke up early. I went into the living room by myself and struggled with this idea. Then this strange feeling of peace came over me. I no longer felt the desire to stay in this new home I helped create and be a part of the church I had so desperately clung to. I woke Matt up and told him what had happened. In a few days, we were driving to the Rockies.

I fell in love with this charming, small town literally between two mountains as we drove through it. We stayed a day, looked at some homes, and tried to figure out what we could do to create an income. Nothing was working, so we drove on to the Springs. We literally drove on the freeway through the Springs. I thought to myself, *This is where I'm supposed to live?* I was not impressed; I was kind of disappointed. I was looking for this small, perfect town full of bright, beautiful colors, big trees, and green grass. I did not see any of this from the freeway.

We continued to drive up into the mountains in our gray, Windstar minivan with an ice chest full of sandwiches and drinks. Brooke, almost three, was coloring in her coloring book. It was about an hour from the Springs. We fell in love with the town. We stayed at a nice motel for a few days. I saw some deer walking in the woods and thought to myself, *This is where I want to be.* A realtor graciously showed us some houses on short notice. We looked at cabins buried in the woods far from town. Nothing stood out. We tried to think of what kind of business this small town needed. We started to get frustrated. Matt liked the idea of opening up a coffee shop. He said I would be great at that. I agreed, but being raised around a restaurant, I knew it took a lot of time and more money. I did not want to do that because I felt my job was to raise Brooke. I was very protective of Brooke; I felt that it was my responsibility to be there for her. This caused conflict between Matt and me.

We left the Rockies feeling confused. Here I thought we were supposed to move there, but nothing was clicking. So we made a deal. Matt said we would go home and put our house up for sale. If it sold, we were supposed to move. Content with the plan, we took what seemed to be a shortcut on the map out of the beautiful woods. It was a scary, dirt road on the edge of the mountain. It made me very nervous and sick. I was praying deep inside, "Please, Lord, bless us not to fall off this mountain!"

> If you make the Lord your refuge, if you make the Most High your shelter, no evil will conquer you; no plague will come near your home. For he will order his angels to protect you wherever you go. They will hold you up with their hands so

you won't even hurt your foot on a stone.
(Psalm 91:9–12 NLT)

It might have been a shortcut, but it took a couple years off my life due to the stress of driving it!

We made it home and called a realtor couple from our church. They were a cute married couple with great enthusiasm. We agreed on a price, and they took some pictures. The house was only on the market for a few days when we got our first offer. It was on a contingency. That meant if the people's house sold, then they would buy ours. We agreed to the offer. A couple days later, we got a new offer, and they wanted us out in thirty days. We agreed to the offer, and our house sold for full price.

We called a realtor in the Rockies. She faxed us some pictures and information on homes. We looked through the homes, looking at all the benefits and negatives. This one house on B Street was perfect: the perfect price, the perfect size, the perfect layout. But it was not in the perfect town. I threw away the listing, thinking it wouldn't work. We were supposed to be in the Springs.

We told our church friends and the pastor we were moving without a house and without a job. I'm sure they thought we were crazy. The pastor gave us the name and number of some good friends who lived in the Springs. Now we had to tell Dad. Oh no! Dad came over for dinner; we sat in the dining room and broke the news to him. I had a spreadsheet of information about the difference between Vegas and the Springs: the lifestyle, job availability, and cost of living. Dad seemed impressed with my homework but not too excited about the move. He did not have any ties to help Matt with his welding business and was not sure we would make it. He left upset. He sold his house next door very quickly too. He moved to his ranch in Utah.

On only faith, we packed up all of our things with the help of a family from church, the Bennetts. They were a nice family that came over and helped us pack up trailers and the back of our new, gray Ford F-350 truck. Yes, gray houses, gray van, and now a gray truck. You would think I liked gray. No, they just happened to be that color. My favorite colors are red and cobalt blue, not gray! They packed us up and helped us drive all the way to our new adventure and unpack our stuff into a storage unit. The friends of our pastor helped us store a brand-new trailer that Matt felt we needed. We all drove back home, had Brooke's third birthday party, and said goodbye to family and friends. Here we were, on our way to a new adventure, not controlled by anyone but ourselves—not crying tears from the past. A new start. Now, it has to get better! Right? Matt's family was only six hours away. They allowed us to use their small camping trailer to live in until we bought a house. We stayed at a campsite.

> And this same God who takes care of me will supply all your needs from his glorious riches, which have been given to us in Christ Jesus. (Philippians 4:19 NLT)

It's funny who God brings into your life at the perfect time. We met some nice couples at the campsite. One retired couple was there to volunteer at a neat Christian place in town. They were so kind and filled with such love for Jesus.

Our new friends, the people pastor recommended, were very welcoming. They invited us over to dinner. They shared crazy stories about living on the side of a mountain. A black bear and her cub moved in under their deck for a while, and deer just roamed through their backyard, eating all kinds of plants and trees.

Matt quickly found a job at a structural steel company. He would go to work while I stayed with Brooke in the camper. After being there a week, I became really sick from the high altitude. I got headaches and became weak and tired. During that same time, we were in our little camper without a television, and September 11 happened. All I heard were air force planes flying over, loudly, shaking our camper. The visitors in the campsite were outside talking to one another about what had just happened. I was scared. I locked the camper and got out my Bible. I read through the whole book of Revelation. Not understanding the words or symbols, I was afraid this was the end. Matt came home, and we went to the home of one of his new co-workers to watch the news. I tried to get ahold of my dad. I did not get an answer. I was worried about him.

Well, not long after September 11, I got a phone call on Matt's cell phone from a policeman. The welding truck that Dad had given Matt had been reported stolen. My dad was now showing us how upset he was that we'd moved. Instead of calling us and talking on the phone, he reported the welding truck stolen. The police officer was very nice. He said we could keep the truck until he came to get it, or we could return it.

When Matt got home from work, I told him what had happened. He got very upset. We packed up our gray truck with food, toys, and Brooke. With both trucks fueled up, we headed to the big city that night to give back the welding truck. It took eleven hours to drive the truck to a small town about four hours from the city of hate. There, a nice man from our former church met us and drove the truck back; he left the truck in the parking lot at Dad's lawyer's office. We turned around that night and drove straight back to our new home, hurt and frustrated but not surprised. You see, Dad's pattern is to attack when his feelings are hurt. Moreover, his feelings were hurt when we moved away. He did not express his feelings in a healthy way but in a destructive way.

After all the crazy commotion settled down, we found a realtor and looked at houses. I had a picture in my head. I could see the house and where it was located all in my mind's eye. This very friendly realtor showed us a few houses in our price range. Nothing was clicking. I was in her office one day, and this print out came about the perfect house that was in the wrong area.

I said, "Oh, that house is perfect, but it is in the wrong town. We are supposed to be in the Springs."

The realtor said we should go look at it. Well, it turned out that it was only ten miles from the Springs. It was perfect! It was a two-story house with an unfinished basement on a two-acre lot. It had four bedrooms and two and a half bathrooms. The kitchen and family room divided off so when people came over unexpectedly, they would not be greeted by a messy room of toys and dirty dishes! I fell in love with it.

There were only two problems with the house. First, it was in a housing community where there were rules that you had to follow-rules like "no one is allowed to park on the side of the road." The rules were hard to agree with. The other problem was the color of the house! Yes, you guessed it! It was another gray house with white trim. Now, we did not let these two issues hold us back. We made an offer, and it was accepted. We closed on our house after only being in the Rockies for a month. That was fast. I thought that with everything coming together we were supposed to be there and things were only going to get better.

> And we know that God causes everything to work together for the good of those who love God and are called according to his purpose for them. For God knew his people in advance, and he chose them to become like his Son, so that his Son would be the firstborn among many brothers and sisters. (Romans 8:28–29 NLT)

So let's do a recap: within three months we had been to and from the Rockies four times, sold our house, lived in a camper, got altitude sickness, were devastated by 9/11, accused of stealing a truck, and bought our perfect house with a white vinyl fence and prairie landscaping! Our new life was going to be full of joy, happiness, peace, no pain, and success! Do you think? Are you worn out from reading about all these problems? Boy, I am! Is there hope in our family's future? Do things get better? No, I am afraid there were more challenges on their way. Though there were many challenges ahead, I am blessed by some loving people only God could have placed in my life when I needed them most.

✑ Now, Everything Will Be Perfect! New State, New Home, and No Parents!

We moved into our house with prairie landscaping. This is just a fancy saying for wild weeds and sagebrush with no grass. We decided not to paint before we moved in. I guess the thought of living in the camper a little longer didn't appeal to us. So the walls were as white as white could be with natural accents of scratches, marks, and moving-in scrapes. Matt and our new friends helped with the big stuff, and Brooke and I were left with everything else while Matt was at work.

This was supposed to be an exciting time for me. I don't remember how my mom got my phone number, but she called and ruined my day. She accused me of lies; I was upset and had to defend myself. Just the normal process. Then I got a phone call from my dad. Boy, they sure knew when to call! He was coming through the Rockies in a week and wanted to stop by and check out our situation. I buried my hurt feelings about the truck and agreed to his visit.

Well, the upcoming visit pushed my productivity! We went and bought a box spring and mattress for our new guest bedroom, and I obsessed over getting everything perfect for his visit. I even took the big truck and went on a search for an oak table and chairs for the kitchen. I found all my cobalt glass and placed it up on the pot shelving in the kitchen and living room. Was I prepared for his visit? The house was, but I was not emotionally ready. Dad and his fourth wife came and checked out everything; they seemed pleased and left. He allowed Matt to have the welding truck back. Things seemed to be back on track. Matt went to work, and I took care of Brooke and fixed up our house. I had no complaints.

We found a Lutheran church in the Springs and went a couple of times. It was an awesome church full of energy, but we felt lost in the size of the church. We felt more comfortable in a smaller church setting. Well, guess what our neighbors down the street were doing? The Hudsons lived three houses down from us and were involved in starting a sister church to the big church we had visited. They wanted to start it out in our little suburb. Wow! God sure knows how to plan things! We became friends and got involved with helping start this new church. We were welcomed into this little church family.

As an outreach one summer, our church gave out free water at a fair. We met some loving people who joined our church family. Pastor Jones and his family moved out to our area from California. He was a retired Lutheran pastor. He agreed to help with the church. His family took my family in as their own. Ally, the Pastor's wife, was so kind and funny. Casey, his adult daughter, was very caring and loving. We would eat dinners together and play games. Pastor would tell us stories and give good advice. They sure were a blessing during those hard challenges. God only knew how much I needed them. Thank you, God!

Matt was very good at impressing people. His goal was to own his own welding business. To be the big guy in control. I stayed home with Brooke. I was very protective and did not feel comfortable leaving her with strangers. We had just moved to this town, and I was not sure who would be a safe sitter. Or was I just hiding behind her because I had become overweight and very insecure about my appearance? Or was it the fact that I had the fear of being in crowds of people? I think all three issues played a part. Matt became very focused on his welding business! His only problem was he did not believe in himself. He had to lie to build himself up. This caused conflict.

> Don't love money; be satisfied with what you have. For God has said, "I will never fail you. I will never abandon you." (Hebrews 13:5 NLT)

❦ I Want To Be the Boss!

Matt was getting tired of working for someone else. Not being in this new territory long, I wanted him to stay with the company for a while and become familiar with the town. I wanted the security of his weekly paycheck. He came home one November day while Mom was visiting and said he had a disagreement with a co-worker and quit. I am not sure what happened; I just know deep down inside Matt wanted his own business and did not consider my opinion. So, our savings started to dwindle as he started his own welding company. He began with himself and his welding truck, doing odd jobs like fixing trailer hitches, building gates for apartment buildings, and making frames for realty signs. Things were stable. The Lord did provide. I was in charge of all the invoices, billings, and advertising. I would go on the internet and find addresses for local businesses that could use a mobile welding man and mail them brochures. It worked for a while, but Matt was not content.

> Without wise leadership, a nation falls; there is safety in having many advisers. (Proverbs 11:14 NLT)

We were supposed to be a team. This was supposed to be our life and our business. He did not take any of my advice into consideration. He wanted to hire a man to help him fabricate gates. I was against it. One reason was because we could not afford to pay him, and the second reason was because Matt and this man would go out and drink together. I did not trust the relationship. Matt hired him anyway. They worked out of our car garage, which was not allowed in our home community rules.

After a while, Matt felt the garage was not big enough, so with me dragging my feet and saying, "You are moving too fast," Matt started to build a nine-hundred-square-foot garage in our backyard. Our budget for the garage was $30,000. Thirty thousand dollars later, the garage was not finished. Learning how to build from my dad, Matt had to overdo everything. It was a large garage with a full bathroom and shower, like Dad's. There were all kinds of outlets, including one for a Jacuzzi. A large heater hung from the ceiling for working during the winter time. There was a large concrete driveway to get to the garage. It was very nice, but Matt was in over his head. He was spending all of our profit from the house we had built and sold as well as the money Dad had given us. It was all slipping away. This made me very uncomfortable. I lost a lot of respect for Matt. He was on a fast-moving train downhill and did not want any advice. This caused conflict.

Well, Matt started to bid for structural steel jobs. He was awarded these jobs that required expensive rental equipment and more employees. This caused a lot of stress. We now had large equipment rental bills, employees, taxes, and insurance to pay. This was not good. Matt was acting like he had all this money, but he didn't. He was spending more than what was coming in.

✂ **Please, God, Bless Me with Another Child**

During all this business stress and commotion, I was still dealing with this strong desire to have another child. I was worried about the age difference between Brooke and a new sibling. I did not want Brooke to grow up without a sister or brother. I did not want her to grow up alone like I had. This also caused emotional stress for me. We had been trying to have another child for three years. I prayed to God, "Please bless me to have another baby." I promised everything I could to God if he would bless me with another child. I finally broke down and went to the doctor. He gave me a prescription that helped me become pregnant. I would later wonder if the side effects of the medicine caused Lilly to have learning disabilities and to be slow in developing motor skills. I was so thankful and excited! Life at home was neither stable nor a healthy place to bring in another child, but I thought it would make things better. I was wrong. Oh, our poor children, please forgive me.

Things only got worse. Matt started to stay out late at night with employees, saying he was working. I was raised in a construction family. I knew jobsites normally shut down around 4:00 p.m. He would not come home until 1:00 or 2:00 a.m. When I would ask him why he was out so late, he would yell at me and make me feel guilty for not trusting him. I did not trust him. This made me physically and emotionally push far away from him. I hid my feelings behind my weight.

I was pregnant, homeschooling Brooke, and doing all the paper work for his business. The business was over $600,000 in debt, and we were barely getting by on fumes and credit cards.

Well, the beautiful baby that I had prayed so hard for came one late November night. A precious baby girl was born! A side note: I do not recommend using castor oil to induce labor! My family was complete now. I was content with two beautiful girls. My mom came down to stay with Brooke while I was in the hospital. Then the nice family from Vegas drove up to meet our new addition. Mom, not able to socialize with our friends, left a couple days after Lilly was born. I became really sick and had to go back to the doctor just days after Lilly was born. I chose to breastfeed Lilly, so she was allowed to come with me. The Bennetts stayed with Brooke. That was hard for me. This was the first time I had been away from Brooke for a long period of time.

I had gotten an infection when I delivered Lilly. I was put on antibiotics and was stuck in the hospital for a couple days. I had cold chills; I would shiver for long periods of time. The nurses would put heated blankets on top of me. I would still shiver, unable to get warm. That was not fun! I was finally released on Saturday, and Lilly was baptized on Sunday, ten days after she was born. She was the first baby baptized in our new little church, and the Bennetts were her godparents. Matt became jealous of Lilly. Lilly liked to be held often, and I was the only one who could feed her. I also believe that I used Lilly to hide from Matt.

He was so manipulating and had such anger. I tried to avoid conflict with him.

∾ We Are Not Big Enough. Let Us Get Bigger!

> For the love of money is the root of all kinds of evil. And some people, craving money, have wandered from the true faith and pierced themselves with many sorrows. (1 Timothy 6:10 NLT)

Well, then came the steel fabricator! This was another one of Matt's ideas—his big shot to make millions of dollars. He buddied up with another business and started to bid on bigger erection jobs that would require a lot of rental equipment and too many employees, which caused more taxes—more money going out and not coming in. I was against it. My dad even pleaded with Matt. He was growing too fast. Matt did not listen. He was consumed with greed. He had his "I can do it" blockers on and felt we were just holding him back.

∾ The People God Brings into Our Lives

Matt became very close to Mr. Bennett. They would talk on the phone all the time. Matt encouraged them to move up to the Springs and start a fabricating business with him. They trusted Matt and his false information, took a leap of faith, and sold their perfect house in Vegas and moved to the Rockies. They came up for a week, looked at some houses, and settled for a modular home. They used the same realtor we adored. The realtor took me out to the home the Bennetts had chosen. It was in a rural area, which would allow them to have horses and a little land for a garden. The house needed a lot of work. I was more interested in another home that was for sale on the same street. I asked to see the house the next day. I thought it was such a better buy.

I was so excited when I called the Bennetts and told them all about it. They asked to see a video of it. I mailed them a video of the house. They agreed and made an offer on the house over the phone without seeing it in person. Wow, what trust they had! They quickly moved into their new house with a couple acres filled with trees and pretty plants, room for horses, and a garden. This home had an extra surprise. The family that sold them the house had prepared for Y2K. They had this shed with a cellar underneath, full of cans of dried food. This was just icing on their cake! A new home and food to survive on for a year! What more do you need?

Matt still had his welding business. He also became business partners with the Bennetts in a prefabricated buildings business. This meant more debt for us. Matt's promises did not come true, and the business shut down. The Bennetts lost their savings. They were still Matt's friends and were there for him.

During this period of time, Matt confessed to Mr. Bennett and then to me that he was a closet alcoholic. He said he would go out and drink in his truck late at night. I was hurt but determined to be supportive. I started to go to

Al-Anon and AA meetings with him. I learned many things in Al-Anon. I learned that not all these things were my fault. They were an excuse for him to drink. I found out that I was an enabler. I started changing. I became more confident. This caused conflict with Matt. He never stopped drinking, although he denied it.

Things got worse. He would stay away for days. I found out at the end that he was going to casinos to gamble large amounts of money and to strip bars with his employees. He would pay his employees to party with him because he knew I kept track of the time cards. He called late one night, very upset, on his way to his dad's house, six hours away. He said he had been somewhere and had gotten in a fight with a man. He'd beaten up the man pretty badly. The man was taken away in the ambulance. Matt was afraid and was running home to hide. I called Mr. Bennett. He found Matt and talked him into coming home.

⬵ The Bible Says to Respect Your Husband. Does that Mean Love Him?

Knowing that Matt was drinking and lying about it, I stopped questioning him when I smelled it on his breath. He had a way of turning it around and making me feel like it was my fault—like I was crazy even though I could smell the alcohol. He really pressured me to take anti-depression medication. I was against it. I had seen my mom get addicted to prescription drugs, and I didn't want to become like her. I finally broke down from the pressure, and I took anti-depressants for a while. I did not feel any differently. I still had the same problems, and I still cried.

The pills did not stop Matt from drinking. Uncomfortable on the meds, I stopped taking them. I believe my depression was caused by the situation. I would go and hide in my dark closet and cry. I would pray, "God, please change me. Please make me stop causing so much conflict." I thought this was all my fault. I could not understand why I could not trust my husband. I struggled with what love meant. I justified not feeling love for him with this scripture verse:

> So again I say, each man must love his wife as he loves himself, and the wife must respect her husband. (Ephesians 5:33 NLT)

Notice it did not say to love your husband, which is how I justified my feelings. It was not a good way to live. He swore that he loved me so much. He felt that I wasn't in love with him. I struggled with the feeling of love, but I was committed to him and our marriage. I tried to love him but questioned what real love was. I had pushed myself away from him because of his hurtful words and lies. Was this real love? Was a real love supposed to treat you this way? I did not think one should, but I wondered what I was doing wrong to deserve this pain and abuse. The harder I prayed, the more I tried to change, and the worse things seemed to get.

> So stop telling lies. Let us tell our
> neighbors the truth, for we are all parts
> of the same body. (Ephesians 4:25 NLT)

We had now been married for nine years. What was I doing? It was all a lie. I acted as if everything was normal, hiding behind my girls and church. I was in charge of fellowship at church. I organized progressive dinners and picnics, and even organized a large garage sale on our church land. We met at an already established Christian church at 4:00 p.m. each Sunday. The church was trying to save money to build a new church on the land. Land was all it was! We were required to have so many activities on the land each year. So we had a garage sale. It was a way to meet our neighbors in a non-church way. I made flyers to hang around town for people to donate unwanted treasures! You ask people to bring unwanted things and, trust me, they will! The treasures came and came! We stored them on the land in a storage unit. We rented a port-a-potty, set up tents, cooked hamburgers, served drinks, and had a successful garage sale! Boy, did that experience make me grow! Trusting that the Lord would provide stuff and people, what a day! God even blessed the weather until 12:00 p.m. when it started to rain. It is amazing how fast people can move and pack when it is raining!

Well, while all these problems were going on, my mom came to live with us. She sold her house in Oregon and moved in with us. I did not want her to move in, knowing that it would not be a healthy choice for anyone. Matt put a guilt trip on me and made me feel like I needed to take care of her. She moved in, and it was the same old situation. She had not let go of the past. She would bring up all the things in her past and her hate for Dad just about every other night. I would get upset and tell her to let it go.

Although I did not share with Mom how bad things were and what Matt had been doing, she started to figure things out. Matt would talk to her about work; he would say we had a big check coming in. Mom and I both believed him. Mom allowed all her money from selling her house to be invested into Matt's company. Shortly after mom's $17,000 was used to pay bills and payroll, we were forced to file bankruptcy. All the tools and equipment went to auction. Our house was in foreclosure. During this stressful time, my mom still felt the need to turn things around to make her the victim. Matt would cause arguments so he could leave and get drunk. I stayed home and took care of my girls, trying to pretend everything was okay.

One morning, my mom, Matt, and I got into an argument right before our meeting with our bankruptcy lawyer. I loaded up my two girls in our new red Excursion that Brooke named Clifford the Big Red Car. (No, it wasn't gray!) We went to the lawyer's office. Mom is very good at making hateful phone calls and writing hurtful letters. While we were filing for bankruptcy, she called my aunt Molly, crying, telling her what was going on. During the unstable conversation, my mom threatened to kill herself. Molly hung up the phone with Mom and called someone.

An ambulance came and picked Mom up. When we got home, we found out what had happened. Mom went into a mental institution for a few weeks and then they helped her move into an apartment. I never saw my mom again. I regretted using her money. I should have never believed it was going to get better. The business had us so buried. I felt like I was drowning. I believe the Lord will provide me with a way to pay Mom back someday.

I spent a lot of time praying for help, asking God to please provide a miracle. We were about to lose our house and cars and our marriage. I would hide in the closet and cry out to God while the girls would take their afternoon naps. I was very depressed and very desperate.

> O Lord, hear me as I pray; pay attention to my groaning. Listen to my cry for help, my King and my God, for I pray to no one but you. Listen to my voice in the morning, Lord. Each morning I bring my requests to you and wait expectantly. (Psalm 5:1–3 NLT)

When the business shut down and after the auction, Matt had some cash. He was supposed to pay an ex-employee $1,300. He took the Excursion and told me he was meeting him in another town. This was in the afternoon. He did not call me until after midnight. He told me that two people jumped him, took the money, and knocked him out, and he had been lying in the dirt in the back of a gas station for all these hours. The police report was in a different county than where he told me he was going.

The ambulance that he called to come pick him up was in a different county than the police report. I met him at the hospital in the Springs. When he walked out of the hospital, his shirt was torn, and he had a scratch on his chest and a big knot on his head. The medical report said he had a concussion. I did not know the man who walked out of the hospital that night. He would not look me in the eye. He was not the man I thought I knew. He was different, distant, and full of anger. I do not know what happened that night. Was he really jumped? Did he go to a casino and gamble it all away, and then try to cover it up with the story? I do not know, and I probably do not want to know what really happened.

> My enemies cannot speak a truthful word. Their deepest desire is to destroy others. Their talk is foul, like the stench from an open grave. Their tongues are filled with flattery. O God, declare them guilty. Let them be caught in their own traps. Drive them away because of their many sins, for they have rebelled against you. (Psalm 5:9–10 NLT)

∾ Good Friday Was a Cold, Dark Day

Matt got a job with a welding company that did a lot of work out of town. He would go away with this company, stay in motels, and come back on the weekends. This provided some money for us to get by. Nevertheless, it did not relieve the stress. Matt was hiding something. I could sense it but did not dare confront him. Matt was getting ready to leave for work, and the doorbell rang. It was a wife of an ex-employee. She was very angry. I answered the door. She told me that Matt had been using her husband to pick up women for him. Shocked and unsure what to say, I said, "I am sorry." Matt was listening in the kitchen. I shut the door, and he came out; he denied it and headed off to work. I was already numb inside and was just trying to survive. I wanted to believe him, but deep down, I had a lot of doubt. Matt would stay away for long periods of time. He would say he was going to see his dad.

While he was gone, I started selling things around the house to buy food and diapers. I sold my kitchenAid, pictures, furniture, clothes, and anything that we did not need. It was very humbling to sit in the garage and have people go through my stuff, buying it for a quarter or a dollar. I was praying for enough money to buy food.

> The high and lofty one who lives in eternity, the Holy One, says this: "I live in the high and holy place with those whose spirits are contrite and humble. I restore the crushed spirit of the humble and revive the courage of those with repentant hearts. (Isaiah 57:15 NLT)

Matt promised Brooke that he would stay home for three days during Easter. All four of us were in the Excursion on our way to Good Friday church services. Matt was insisting that we go and trade the Excursion in for another vehicle. I thought he was crazy. I did not think anyone would give us a loan. He had bought a little white junk car that was a stick shift to drive to work and home. I said to him, "Why don't I learn how to drive a stick shift, and I will drive the little car. We will turn in the Excursion, and you can drive the welding truck until they come to repo it." He did not like that idea. He was very insistent on getting a different vehicle. He got so upset, he turned around and headed home. I told him if he left us on Easter that he should not come back.

Brooke was crying in the back, "Dad, you promised you would stay for three days. You promised." He went into the house, packed his things, and left. As I cried, I called my pastor. He said he would come over later. I loaded my girls back up and headed to Good Friday service. I hid all the pain deep down inside so no one at church could see me breaking. We sat far in the back of the church. As I walked down and hammered my nail into the cross, I begged God for help. "Please, Lord, have mercy on my girls and me!"

We came home, and I talked to the pastor and his family. He said we needed to schedule a meeting with Matt to try to work this out. The meeting was set for the next Friday at our house. I went on and tried to act normal. I made dinner for the girls and me. Saturday, I played with the kids and prepared for Easter. On Easter morning, we got dressed in our Easter dresses and went to church. I was in charge of the Easter egg hunt for the kids. We hid eggs in the small basement of the church. I thought the kids had fun. Dad called that day to wish us a happy Easter. Brooke was talking to him. She told him that Daddy left us. My dad asked to talk to me. I broke down crying. He told me that I was a good wife and someday I would find a good man. I could not believe it. This was the same man who years before had told me that if I didn't get my act together, I would be a single mom on welfare. He had made it seem so bad to be divorced, and now he was saying I was better off without Matt. Thank you, God, for letting me hear those words. Dad said that he was going to be coming through and that the girls and I should get away for a while. I told him that I would let him know what happened at the meeting with Matt.

That next Friday came. The pastor came, and his daughter came along to watch the girls upstairs. We sat down at the dining room table. The pastor talked for a little bit about marriage and how the stress of the bankruptcy can cause these feelings. I asked for forgiveness for everything I had ever done wrong as a wife. I told Matt that I would pack up all our things, put them in storage, and go live in motels while he worked. I would homeschool the girls. I got up crying and went to the bathroom. Crying, I prayed to Jesus, begging for help. This strange feeling came over me, and I knew he was not going to stay. I simply said out loud, "God's will be done," and walked back into the living room. Matt said he was shocked and said he did not expect this, but he would have to stick with plan A, which was to leave and get a divorce.

The pastor and his daughter left. It was just Matt, the girls, and me. I was holding Lilly on my hip. I grabbed onto Matt and begged him not to leave. He told me to stop, and he walked out the door. I went into the kitchen, crying, still holding Lilly. I screamed at the top of my lungs, "Noooooooooooooo!" I then tried to put myself back together, praying to Jesus for help, saying to myself, "It will be okay." I stopped crying. The next day, I packed our bags. I had just enough money to get to Denver, where I was supposed to meet Dad. We spent three weeks with Dad. I read Dr. James C. Dobson's book, *Love Must Be Tough.* It made a lot of sense. It helped me work through many issues.

Dad said that he would help me only if I left the Rockies. He was afraid that if I stayed, I would allow Matt to use Dad's money and me. He gave me two choices: his ranch in Utah or a new place in Iowa. I had bad memories of the ranch, so I chose a new place, a new adventure. When the three weeks were up, we drove back to the Rockies with the plan to move out of the house. We arrived late at night in front of that perfect house that I was supposed to live in. I went in and looked around. The next morning, Matt and I were scheduled to go to bankruptcy court. I borrowed a neighbor's car and went to the courthouse. Dad went to the emergency room. He had stepped out of the motor home wrong and fractured a part of his foot. They put his foot in a walking cast. Then Dad and his wife went straight to the U-Haul place and rented a large moving truck. He did not allow his broken foot to slow him down. Pride and stubbornness can cause extra pain!

I met Matt at the courthouse. I tried to act very calm and strong. When bankruptcy court was over, I walked out of the courthouse, Matt wanted to talk. I did not see the point in talking and left. Ladies from church had found boxes, tape, and about eight people to help pack and load the moving truck. We had most of the house packed in a large U-Haul by 4:00 p.m. that afternoon.

> Share each other's burdens, and in this way obey the law of Christ. (Galatians 6:2 NLT)

I am so thankful to God for the friends He provided when I needed them the most. Can you imagine a whole house packed up in one day? Some of these people were in their sixties and seventies. We were all worn out! Matt never came by that day to say goodbye to his girls. He called a couple times and promised he would come see them in the summer, but he never did. Dad took us out to dinner that night. This was my last night in a place I thought I had been called to live in by God. I had some mixed emotions. We came back to the motor home and tried to go to sleep. This was a scary time for me. I was leaving a life that was not stable, but it was all I knew. I was more afraid of sinning against God than Matt. My pastor assured me that I was doing the right thing. Matt had abandoned us, and we had no choice but to leave with my dad. We left early the next morning. On the way to our new home, Dad's wife was driving the motor home and Dad was driving the U-Haul. Sitting in the motor home, I started having second thoughts. I did not speak out or tell anyone.

I started praying that the motor home would stop and we could go back. I was scared of what was going to happen next. I was going to be a single mom. How was I going to take care of these girls? I was scared about Brooke having to go to public school and putting Lilly in daycare all day. This was not how I wanted to raise these girls. I felt it was my job to be there for my girls, not apart from them all day. How was I going to provide for them?

☙ I Would Have Never Left; I Am Thankful He Did

> But if the husband or wife who isn't a believer insists on leaving, let them go. In such cases the believing husband or wife is no longer bound to the other, for God has called you to live in peace. (1 Corinthians 7:15 NLT)

Well, we got to our new destination, unpacked, and started planning the next step. Dad took me house hunting. Dad did not want a fixer-upper because he would be the one doing all the repairs. We found a somewhat new house that was perfect. It had a nice kitchen, two bedrooms, one bathroom, and a full basement perfect for daycare. I got all the information I needed to start a daycare business out of my home. I became a registered daycare provider.

> There are "friends" who destroy each other, but a real friend sticks closer than a brother. (Proverbs 18:24 NLT)

Taylor found me at my new destination, as she always did. When I moved to the Panhandle, she found me. When I moved to Vegas, she not only found me, she came and celebrated Brooke's birthday with us. When I moved to the Rockies, she came and visited us. I am ashamed to say I was not on my best behavior at that time. I was so deep in my own pain that I was unable to be a good friend. This last move came so quickly, I was unable to inform her. She sure did track me down this time. She remembered my dad's name, looked up his information, and called him. He gave her my new number. I will never understand why she still, to this day, is my friend. I have moved so many times. I have pushed away from so many people. She still finds me! It just boggles my mind. I guess God is like that. We push away when we are ashamed, or not doing things right, or if we are afraid, sad, or angry. God just finds us and sticks around. He comforts us when we are in those dark places, and He takes us out of situations that are not healthy and dangerous. Thank you, God!

> The Lord is my shepherd; I have all that I need. He lets me rest in green meadows; he leads me beside peaceful streams. He renews my strength. He guides me along right paths, bringing honor to his name. Even when I walk through the darkest valley, I will not be afraid, for you are close beside me. Your rod and your staff protect and comfort me. You prepare a feast for me in the presence of my enemies. You honor me by anointing my head with oil.

> My cup overflows with blessings. Surely
> your goodness and unfailing love will
> pursue me all the days of my life, and I
> will live in the house of the Lord forever.
> (Psalm 23 NLT)

In our new place where lots of corn grows, I was finally able to plant that garden that I had been praying about for many years. The weight I had been struggling to lose for too many years began to come off. Eighty-five painful pounds! I discovered how to jumpstart a riding lawnmower and check the oil. I learned not to plant three rows of zucchini unless you want to feed a whole town! I popped a tire on a wheelbarrow, but I still conquered the two tons of rock trying to landscape my new home. It just takes one scoop at a time!

I started to take control of my life. My girls and I are healing slowly.

Having a daycare out of my home allowed me to be home with my girls.

My hemorrhage problem did come back after moving and taking on a new life. I became overworked and stressed out. I tried to control it but failed. I was afraid to go to the hospital. Who would take care of my girls? Dad was far away at his ranch in Utah. Dad had called me one day and asked if I had mowed his property in Iowa. I said no. He was upset and asked why not. I broke down crying and told him I had been hemorrhaging nonstop for six weeks and felt really weak. He got off the phone with me and called his mother-in-law who lived in town. She came over to check on me. When she came over, my house was not in order and the girls were watching TV; I was lying on the floor with my feet up on the couch. She said, "I think you should go to the hospital."

I said, "Okay!" with tears in my eyes. I knew it had gone too far. She took me to the hospital. I stayed in the hospital all alone that night, praying that my girls were okay. This amazing thing happens when you become a mother. Your feelings take a back seat to your children. Lilly, who was two, had never been away from me at nighttime. I was worried that she would cry all night. I cried as I prayed that the Lord would comfort her while I was gone. I did not want my girls to feel scared or abandoned. When I was fourteen years old I had to have two bags of blood, but now I had to have six bags of blood and plasma pumped back into my tired, worn-out body. As I watched the blood slowly go through the IV, I prayed that the Lord would have mercy upon me and help me through these hard times. I was released from the hospital with a prescription and a bottle of red iron tablets. I did feel a little better but still very weak. A scary experience like that can make you take better care of yourself!

✂ God Got Us out Just in Time!

What happened to Matt? Well, I am thankful and believe it was by God's grace that we were able to get away as fast as we did. Matt only got worse and made some very bad choices. He will be spending most of my children's lives in prison. I remember it was late at night, and he called my house, drunk. He was driving around in his car. He told me he had done something very bad. He told me I would read about it in the newspapers. He said he was going to kill himself. I said, "No, you are not; you love your girls too much." I told him to go turn himself in to the police. He agreed and hung up the phone. I went to bed, not sure what to believe. I got up the next morning, pretending everything was fine. I got the girls dressed, and we went to a summer parade. I felt very numb inside with worried thoughts going through my mind, praying that God would help me take care of these girls.

When we got home from the parade, there were two messages on the answering machine. One was from Matt's good friend, Mr. Bennett, and one was from Pastor Jones. Both informed me that Matt had turned himself in for a horrible crime. He had dragged a woman from a strip club into a field, beat her, and then straggled her to death. I later found out that he confessed to killing two other women. It boggles my mind how I stayed so calm. I did not have any feeling inside. I guess I had endured so much pain I had become numb. I am thankful that my girls and I were not there and harmed. I pray for the families that were caused pain by Matt. I pray they find peace through Jesus Christ. I pray my two girls will not be emotionally traumatized by his actions. I do not have any hate for Matt. I feel sorry for him. Because of his actions, he has missed out on two beautiful girls growing up.

And do not bring sorrow to God's Holy Spirit by the way you live. Remember, he has identified you as his own, guaranteeing that you will be saved on the day of redemption. Get rid of all bitterness, rage, anger, harsh words, and slander, as well as all types of evil behavior. Instead, be kind to each other, tenderhearted, forgiving one another, just as God through Christ has forgiven you. (Ephesians 4:30–33 NLT)

ଚ What Happened to My Parents?

My mom moved back to Vegas and lived with my grandma for a year. During that year, she called the cops in my new town and said I was in danger; it scared me to death when the cops came knocking on my door. She has also put several ads in the local newspaper with pictures of the girls, saying, "Grammy not dead, just left behind." After living with her mother and father in a trailer for a year, they all got into a fight, and she moved out. She moved in with an old neighbor from her past. She still sends hurtful letters to me, reminding me of all the pain I have caused her. She sends boxes of gifts to my girls in the mail. I question her motives behind the gifts. Are they just gifts or is she trying to buy their love? I pray she would let go of all the hate and anger and do something positive with the rest of her life. She was such a gifted designer with such confidence. She just got stuck in the hurt, lies, and hate. She was not able to get over all the hard things that happened in her life. I do not have any hate for my mom. I love her. I pray she lets go of the strongholds that are keeping her captive. I pray she finds peace through Jesus Christ.

My experience with my ex-husband's welding company has made me understand my dad more. Dad had so much pressure to make his construction company successful. It took a lot out of him. It caused a lot of stress. The divorce and my mom's mean games did not help matters either. I am very thankful that God provided me with a loving father when Matt left. The words he said on the phone were so kind. I needed him, and he was there. I am so thankful for my dad. That tough Irish man fills up with tears when he speaks of how much he loves his half-breed rent-a-kid.

I have never met my biological parents. My mom tried to find my biological dad during the long custody battle. Her purpose was only to hurt my dad. I have no hate towards the people that gave me up for adoption. God blessed me with parents who tried with all of their hearts to love and take care of me. As a kid, I always felt special. I pray God blesses my biological parents with peace.

&o The Mother I Desperately Need.

It was Mother's Day recently. They were giving a tribute to mothers at church. It made me think about the special women God has placed in my life. My mom gave me the desire to be creative. My grandma gave me a place of peace. My Aunt Molly loved me just the way I was. The true Italian woman taught me it was okay to be a girl. Dad's fourth wife taught me that girls could be strong. A new special friend, Robin, met me when I was broken, lost, and in so much pain. Through her prayers, time, and guidance, Robin has helped me heal. She has helped me overcome my fears and find peace. I am so thankful for the people God has placed in my life during the time I desperately needed them. God is a good, good father!

☙ What Would One Learn from All These Challenges?

> For I can do everything through Christ, who gives me strength. (Philippians 4:13)

My girls and I are doing well. We are healing from all the pain. I have learned that I can make it on my own. I am a good person, and I am not crazy! I should have never tried to fix a bad situation with another one by getting married. It did not help the matter at all. I am so thankful for my two beautiful girls that God has blessed me with. I have tried so hard to be the best mom I can be for them. I am thankful for the challenges and experiences in my life. If I had not gone through all the pain and challenges, I would not have reached out and searched for God. Please, God, no more pain!

> Remember your promise to me; it is my only hope. Your promise revives me; it

> comforts me in all my troubles. (Psalm
> 119:49–50 NLT)

> The righteous person faces many
> troubles, but the Lord comes to the rescue
> each time. (Psalm 34:19 NLT)

You would think that my faith would have been broken through all of these challenges. Amazingly, it has strengthened me. There were times in my life when the only things I had were God, the love of Jesus, and the hope of being in heaven one day. When I look back on that dark day Matt left, I no longer see the pain; I see Jesus looking through the window with His arms wide open. I understand that Jesus was there with me, feeling my pain.

When I could not handle the pain, I just wanted to go and hide in a dark place and cry. Even though it was dark, I was not alone. There have been times when I have been angry with God, not understanding why He even allowed me to be born. I felt that I was a mistake, looking at all the pain I've caused and felt. *What is my purpose? Where is Wednesday's Place?* Then something happens, or someone comes by and says something that gives me that comfort, that assurance that I am loved by God so much that He gave His one and only Son to die for me. Wow! Now that is a reason to live! Is it my purpose to go through all this pain so I can say that even though I have had many challenges, the only thing that has never changed is God's love for me? He has always been there for me, even when I have pushed Him away. I now see all the times that God protected me, shielded me from even worse things. God has put people in my life to teach me about love, sacrifice, giving, and having faith. I am no longer a rent-a-kid but the accepted, beloved, adopted daughter of the King of Kings!

> I will exalt you, Lord, for you rescued me. You refused to let my enemies triumph over me. O Lord my God, I cried to you for help, and you restored my health. You brought me up from the grave, O Lord. You kept me from falling into the pit of death. Sing to the Lord, all you godly ones! Praise his holy name. For his anger lasts only a moment, but his favor lasts a lifetime! Weeping may last through the night, but joy comes with the morning. When I was prosperous, I said, "Nothing can stop me now!" Your favor, O Lord, made me as secure as a mountain. Then you turned away from me, and I was shattered. I cried out to you, O Lord. I begged the Lord for mercy, saying, "What will you gain if I die, if I sink into the grave? Can my dust praise you? Can it tell of your faithfulness? Hear me, Lord, and have mercy on me. Help me, O Lord." You have turned my mourning into joyful dancing. You have taken away my clothes of mourning and clothed me with joy, that I might sing praises to you and not

be silent. O Lord my God, I will give you
thanks forever! (Psalm 30 NLT)

God is real and He does love you with all of His heart.
Look at how many chances He gives us to realize we need
Him. This world is so hard and full of such pain, but there
is hope through the blood of Jesus. Thank you, God, for
not giving up on me!

May I dance and sing for you, O Lord, and bring you
glory!

About the Author

Wednesday Grace is now married to a big teddy bear who has taught her that not everyone leaves. She has been blessed with two beautiful daughters who have taught her how to love. Three words have been spoken over Wednesday tears, fears, and cheers. She's cried many tears on her journey. Now, after years of overcoming her fears, she wants to cheer over what God has done in her life! Wednesday Grace wants to help others who are going through their own tears and fears. She wants to share how God held her hand while she found her place—her purpose.

Printed in the United States
By Bookmasters